THE
LITTLE
BOOK
OF THE
COTSWOLDS

GILLIAN BROOMHALL

WITH ILLUSTRATIONS BY GWEN BURNS

The
History
Press

For John, my soul mate

First published 2011

The History Press
The Mill, Brimscombe Port
Stroud, Gloucestershire, GL5 2QG
www.thehistorypress.co.uk

British Library Cataloguing in Publication Data.
A catalogue record for this book is available from the British Library.

ISBN 978 0 7524 5444 3
Typesetting and origination by The History Press
Printed in the EU for The History Press.

CONTENTS

INTRODUCTION &
ACKNOWLEDGEMENTS

As anyone who loves the Cotswolds will appreciate, attempting to squeeze the legion delights of the region into a 'Little Book' is an impossible task. Not only are the Cotswolds devastatingly beautiful, they're stuffed to the prehistoric gills with drama; they ooze culture and intrigue; and the fascinating saints and sinners who've checked in and out over the centuries could quite easily fill several books of their own.

That said, I hope I've managed to cram enough of my personal favourites into this snapshot of Cotswold life to inspire you to explore further, indulge in a little time travel, support a conservation project, perhaps even learn to build a dry stone wall or venture a few steps with the Morris – but most important of all, celebrate the wonderful Cotswolds.

Special thanks to the Cotswolds Conservation Board (cotswoldsaonb. org.uk) – particularly Land Management Officer Mark Connelly for his encyclopaedic knowledge and discerning appreciation of the Cotswolds; Folk music researcher and performer Gwilym Davies (cmarge.demon.co.uk/gwilym/) for his expertise and the Winchcombe play excerpt; Mary Bliss MBE, Will Willans (Tower Master, Bath Abbey), Tower Captain Peter Holden and the bell ringers of St John Baptist, Cirencester, and Tower Captain Edward Cribley and the bell ringers of Christ Church, Chalford; Andrew Young & Helen Crabtree of the Letter Box Study Group (lbsg.org); Cotswolds and Forest of Dean Tourism (cotswolds.com) for much of the information about films; the Cotswold Sheep Society (cotswoldsheepsociety. co.uk); Ralph Windle (ralphwindle.com) for permission to quote from his lovely poem, 'Cotswold Sheep'; The Churches Conservation Trust (visitchurches.org.uk); Charles Martell; Gloucestershire Orchard Group (gloucestershireorchardgroup.org.uk); the endlessly helpful staff/volunteers of the region's visitor information centres, Gloucestershire Archives, Nailsworth, Stow-on-the-Wold and Stroud libraries, Nailsworth Archives, Dursley Heritage Centre and Wotton-under-Edge Heritage Centre; the many wonderful churchwardens, PCC secretaries and church guides around the Cotswolds.

I am also indebted to the following: Paul Adkins, David Bishop, Stan Burrage, Frank Byrne, Jim Chapman, Johnny Coppin, Stuart Cummings, Robin Dale (National Hedgelaying Society), Terry Day, Carl Evans, Dennis Gardner, Edward Jenner Museum (Berkeley), Ann Haigh, Dr Anthony Hammond, Joe Henson, Laurence Hitchins, Richard Ingles, Jean Jeffries, Charles Keen, Philip Lee-Woolf, Ian Macintosh, Peter Morris, Paul Nash, Daphne Neville, Brian Riley, Sarah Schenk, Anne Stabler, Vic Sutton, Bob Woodward, Avon Wildlife Trust, Bath Preservation Trust, Bisley Blue Coat Church of England Primary School, Bourton Rovers Football Club, Broadway Tower, Canterbury Cathedral, Chedworth Roman Villa (NT), Cheltenham Art Gallery & Museum, Cheltenham Borough Council, Claverton Pumping Station group, Cleeve Common Board of Conservators, Corinium Museum (Cirencester), Cotswold Canals Trust, Cotswold Water Park Society, the Dry Stone Walling Association of Great Britain, The Ebworth Centre, Ecotricity, Gloucester City Museum and Art Gallery, Gloucestershire Morris Men, Gloucestershire Wildlife Trust, Holst Birthplace Museum (Cheltenham), Intermusica, Katherine Mansfield Society, National Grid, Natural History Museum, Naunton Village Trust, Robert Dover's Games Society, St Paul's Cathedral, Salisbury Racecourse, Sheepscombe Cricket Club, Stanway Estate, Stowell Park Estate Ltd, Tetbury Woolsack Committee, 'Thankful Villages' (Norman Thorpe, Tom Morgan & Rod Morris), The Bathurst Estate & Cirencester Park, The Croquet Association, The Finzi Trust, The Metropolitan Museum of Art (NY), the Museum in the Park (Stroud), The Oxfordshire Museum (Woodstock), The RAF Down Ampney Association, The Tolsey Museum (Burford), Victoria and Albert Museum, Violet Needham Society, Wellington Aviation Museum, Cal Williams (Randwick Wap Committee), Woodstock Mock Mayor Corporation, and all those it has not been possible to list by name.

Finally, a huge thank you to Gwen Burns for her delightful illustrations.

Gillian Broomhall, 2011

1

THE COTSWOLDS – NATURALLY

COTSWOLD BOOT CAMP

The Cotswolds extend approximately 90 miles through six different counties – Gloucestershire, Oxfordshire, Somerset, Warwickshire, Wiltshire and Worcestershire.

The Cotswolds Area of Outstanding National Beauty (AONB) is a protected landscape of national importance. Managed by the Cotswolds Conservation Board (consisting of fifteen local authorities, three unitary authorities and four county councils), it is the largest of the thirty-eight AONBs in England and Wales, covering 790 square miles. A team of over 350 Cotswold Voluntary Wardens (established 1968) supports the Cotswolds Conservation Board. In 2009/10 alone, they clocked up a staggering 43,652 recorded hours.

The Cotswolds has eighty-nine Special Sites of Scientific Interest (SSSI) including thirty-six Geological SSSI sites, five European Special Areas of Conservation and three National Nature Reserves – Cotswold Commons and Beechwoods National Nature Reserve; Bredon Hill and Wychwood Forest.

There are some 3,000 miles of public footpath in the Cotswolds, including two national trails – the Cotswold Way, covering 102 miles from the Market Hall at Chipping Campden in the north to Bath Abbey in the south, and a small section of the Thames Path. There are also literally hundreds of guided walks/riding/cycling trails and events run by such organisations as the CCB, the National Trust, the Wildlife Trusts, as well as private organisations and some local authorities.

Despite the old adage 'Tis as long in coming as Cotteswold barley', over 80 per cent of the Cotswold landscape is agricultural. Its principal crops are barley, grass, field beans, oilseed rape and wheat. The region's main industry is tourism.

DON'T LOOK DOWN

The Cotswold Hills form part of an outcrop of Jurassic rock running from the Dorset coast to the coast of Yorkshire.

The geology of the Cotswolds dramatically characterises the region – its underlying oolitic limestone has been widely used as building stone over the centuries. Closely observed, the stone resembles tiny fish eggs, hence the Greek term oolite or 'egg stone'.

The highest point of the Cotswolds is at Cleeve Hill (also known as Cleeve Cloud) which rises 1,083ft above sea level. Other top spots include:

Birdlip Hill	Kelston Round Hill (near Bath)
Brailes Hill	Leckhampton Hill
Bredon Hill	Meon Hill
Broadway Hill	Stinchcombe Hill
Cutsdean Hill	Painswick Beacon
Dover's Hill	Tog Hill (near Bath)
Ebrington Hill	Uley Bury
Fish Hill (near Broadway)	

Perhaps not so significant for height, the following hills nevertheless deserve a name-check:

Awkward Hill (Bibury)
Bear Hill (Rodborough)
Hunger Hill (near Dursley)
Nailsworth 'W' – a serpentine thriller that gets the better of many a cyclist, not to mention a few engines, at the classic reliability trials held off-road (straight up the side) here every winter since before the Second World War
Nibley Knoll

Pancake Hill (Chedworth)
Scar Hill (Minchinhampton)
Solsbury Hill (near Bath) – as in the Peter Gabriel song of the same name
Smallpox Hill (Uley)

WATER & WIND

Let fancy lead, from Trewsbury Mead,
With hazel fringed, and copsewood deep,
Where scarcely seen, through brilliant green,
Thy infant waters softly creep

Thomas Love Peacock (died 1866)

A single stone marks the official source of England's longest river, the Thames, which rises at Trewsbury Mead near Kemble – although some quote Seven Springs as its true source (also has a stone).

Cotswold places with names linked to rivers/tributaries include:

Ampney (a brook) – Down Ampney, Ampney Crucis, Ampney St Mary, Ampney St Peter
Avon – Avening
Churn – South Cerney, North Cerney, Cerney Wick, Cirencester
Coln – Coln St Aldwyns, Coln St Dennis, Coln Rogers
Dunt (a stream) – Duntisbourne Abbots, Duntisbourne Rouse, Duntisbourne Leer, Middle Duntisbourne
Frome – Frampton (Mansell)
Leach – Northleach, Eastleach Turville, Eastleach Martin, Lechlade
Evenlode (immortalised in verse by Hilaire Belloc) – Evenlode, Bledington
Windrush – Windrush
The rivers Leach, Coln and Cole all meet at the Thames' highest navigable point at Lechlade.

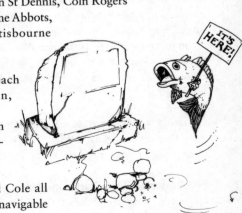

The majority of Cotswold rivers flow into the Thames. The river Avon branches at Sherston and Tetbury, meeting at Malmesbury and flowing by way of Bath and Bristol to join the River Severn at Avonmouth.

Cotswold rivers are classed as salmonid, as some contain native brown trout.

The Cotswolds are a major aquifer supplying the south-east.

An ongoing restoration project by the Cotswold Canals Partnership (established in 2001) aims to restore two historic Cotswold canals, thus reconnecting the mighty Thames and Severn rivers after more than seventy years. The 7-mile Stroudwater Navigation (opened in 1779, closed to navigation in 1954) linked the River Severn with Stroud and was one of the earliest in England. The 29-mile Thames & Severn Canal (completed in 1789, finally closed by 1933) connected with the Thames near Lechlade and the end of the Stroudwater Navigation at Wallbridge. Its ambitious 2-mile tunnel between Sapperton and Coates was the longest in the country at the time.

Having lain derelict for fifteen years, the Claverton Pumping Station (completed 1813) near Bath, re-opened in 1978 following restoration by volunteers from the Kennet & Avon Canal Trust. Machinery enclosed in a beautiful pump house made of Bath Stone, including a huge 24ft-wide waterwheel, generates enough power from the River Avon to pump nearly 100,000 gallons of water per hour back up to the canal, which is situated 48ft above. The pump was designed to replenish water loss in the 9-mile pound between Bath and Bradford-on-Avon.

Cotswold streams provide vital habitats for a wide variety of wildlife including the caddis fly, dipper, white-clawed crayfish, water vole and otter (found principally on the Thames tributaries).

The Cotswold Water Park, situated at the head of the Thames Valley, consists of over 150 lakes formed by gravel extraction, which first began over half a century ago. As well as providing a range of sport and leisure activities, the 40 square-mile area provides a haven for wildlife including otters, water vole, wildflower meadows, dragonflies, and high numbers of wintering waterfowl.

The good folk of Bourton-on-the-Water traditionally site their village Christmas tree in the middle of the River Windrush, which flows through the centre of the village.

The Cotswolds' first and only wind turbine to date stands at Nympsfield. Installed on Friday, 13 December 1996, it produces 1.1 million units of green electricity per annum. It was also the first wind turbine installed in Gloucestershire, as well as the largest in Britain at the time.

TREE-MENDOUS

The Cotswolds is significant for its veteran trees and ancient woodland, boasting internationally important beech and yew woods. In fact, woodland accounts for 10.1 per cent of the Cotswolds AONB – there are 20,657 hectares of it within the Cotswolds. Fine examples can be found at Cranham Woods, the ancient oak/ash woodland to the north of Bath, and the ancient hazel and beech woodland of Chedworth Woods. Buckholt Wood near Painswick covers 247 acres and forms part of the Cotswold Commons and Beechwoods National Nature Reserve.

Frith Wood (also known as Morley Penistan Memorial) near Painswick is beautiful ancient beech woodland. Cared for by Gloucestershire Wildlife Trust (GWT), its beech trees are thought to have come from seed planted after the Napoleonic Wars, possibly from Belgium, while the ancient woodland of Midger Wood, near Hillesley (GWT) features distinctive mature field maples and supports many forms of wildlife, including over twenty species of butterfly, the yellow-necked mouse and the (not so common) common dormouse.

The start of a series of events celebrating the 900th anniversary of the creation of the Royal Park of Woodstock by Henry I in AD 1110 was marked by the release of 900 biodegradable birthday balloons from the town's square. Almost 1,500 trees have since been planted on the Blenheim Estate as part of an ongoing project to create a new community woodland, featuring harvestable coppice trees such as hazel and ash, as well as 'high forest' trees chosen especially for the benefit of future generations.

A tree on Rodborough Common, near Stroud, is known locally as the 'Dog Christmas Tree' due to its annual decoration by owners in memory of their pets, while the famous knarled 'Tortworth Chestnut' (situated on the edge of the Cotswolds near Wotton) still stands in a field next to the church of St Leonard, Tortworth. One of the accompanying plaques states, 'This Tree Supposed To Be Six Hundred Years Old 1st Jany. 1800', followed by the verse:

May Man Still Guard thy Venerable form
From the Rude Blasts, and Tempestous Storm
Still mayest thou Flourish through Succeeding time
And Last, Long Last, the Wonder of the Clime

Meanwhile, some 32 miles away at Cleeve Common, a single windswept beech must be the highest tree in the Cotswolds, standing at a lofty 317 metres.

The mammoth semi-circular yew hedge that separates Cirencester's mansion house (a private residence) from the town centre is believed to have been planted in the early 1700s by the first Earl Bathurst. Measuring 40ft high and 33ft wide at the base, the hedge is trimmed every August from a hydraulic platform. The resulting fresh clippings are sent away for use in the production of anti-cancer drugs.

Beautiful old yew trees stand sentinel in many a Cotswold churchyard, including the famous ninety-nine trees at St Mary's, Painswick. Tradition has it that the devil won't allow any more to grow, which is probably just as well. In view of the expense of their upkeep, a church official recently came up with an inspired 'Sponsor a Yew' scheme – over-subscribed in no time at all. Each much-loved tree now has a marker detailing its sponsors – from individuals and local businesses, to the residents of an entire street.

APPLES & GRAPES

Seven rare Cotswold apples:

Ampney Red (Ampney Crucis)
Gloucester Royal (Dursley)
Jill Jeffries (Siddington)
Northland Seedling (Tetbury)
Lodgemore Nonpareil (Stroud)
Siddington Russet (Siddington)
Rissington Redstreak (possibly Great Rissington)

In an effort to counteract a dramatic loss of Gloucestershire orchards over the last fifty years, the Gloucestershire Orchard Group (founded in 2001), among others, is working hard to help get all the region's heritage apple varieties back into the landscape via schools, gardens, councils and community projects. More than 750 traditional county orchards have also been surveyed for the Peoples' Trust for Endangered Species (PTES).

It was Charles Martell (of *Wallace & Gromit*/Stinking Bishop cheese fame) who originally started surveying Gloucestershire fruit orchards in the late 1980s, interviewing their owners to record and save the fast disappearing native fruit varieties. Rather than the dozen or so apples he expected, an amazing 106 varieties have so far been re-discovered, all of which feature in the National Council for the Conservation of Plants and Gardens (NCCPG) collection on his farm at Dymock. A further eighty-plus have been documented but are still technically lost.

Meanwhile, a Mother Tree Orchard (trees maintained as bushes to give plenty of graft wood for propagation) duplicating the original collection has been established by the Gloucestershire County Council at Uckington, near Cheltenham (not open to the public), enabling other complete or partial collections to be planted around the county, including a museum orchard at the GOG Orchard & Rural Skills Centre, Brookthorpe. Orchard training courses, blossom trails, apple, pear and plum days, as well as many other juicy events are also held throughout the year with several traditional apple varieties now sold at local farmers' markets.

The Cotswolds' only vinery is represented by the Bow-in-the-Cloud Vineyard in the hamlet of Noah's Ark near Malmesbury (although of course, it's only the second vineyard to be located in the vicinity of Noah's Ark, since Noah himself planted the first).

LIVING ON THE HEDGE

Traditional hedgelaying has been practised for hundreds of years to rejuvenate hedges and encourage new growth. The healthy living hedge provides effective stock control, marks boundaries, protects crops and animals and provides an invaluable natural habitat for insects, small mammals and birds, as well as forming part of our heritage (some hedgerows are hundreds of years old).

Although most hedges are now managed by machinery, the Midland-style of hedgelaying is the traditional form of management in the north Cotswolds. Other parts of the Cotswolds have Southern, Berkeley Vale and Somerset styles of hedgelaying.

The hedgelayer firstly prunes out any deadwood and unwanted plants before cutting two thirds of the way through, near the base of the hedge stems. The cut stems (called 'pleachers') are then laid over at a 45-degree angle (so that the rainwater runs off) and vertically staked with, for example, hazel, ash or hawthorn at about 18in intervals. Finally, the craftsman cleverly weaves a rope-like structure along the top of the stakes using 'heathers' or 'binders' – usually hazel – and the operation is complete. In the course of time, new growth shoots up from the base of the pleached stems, providing a strong and vigorous hedgerow.

Hedgelayers of all ages, from all parts of the country, gather in the Cotswolds each year to battle it out at the North Cotswolds Hedgelaying Competition – a countryside event organised by the Cotswolds Conservation Board in association with the National Hedgelaying Society (Patron HRH The Prince of Wales) to promote this ancient skill. The society's national championship has been held in the Cotswolds on two occasions in recent years.

COTSWOLD FLOWER POWER

The Cotswolds contains over 50 per cent of the UK's total 'Unimproved Jurassic Limestone Grassland' resource – an important habitat for many rare plants. There are over 300 grassland sites totalling some 3,000 ha.

Cleeve Common (a 1,000-acre protected habitat of national importance) represents the largest area of unimproved limestone grassland in Gloucestershire. Many wild flowers can be found on the Common including burnet-saxifrage, horseshoe vetch, bird's foot trefoil and several types of orchid. Due to its areas of Harford Sands capping the jurassic limestone, the Common also has areas of heath species such as heather, heath bedstraw and tormentil – unusual wildflowers for the Cotswolds. The limestone grassland is not the natural habitat, but rather the result of thousands of years of grazing, without which this important environment would eventually revert to scrubland of rough grass, gorse and hawthorn. A massive grant-funded project, involving 5,800 metres of pipe, is currently underway to provide a reliable source of water for the Common's livestock (cattle and sheep), thus ensuring the sustainability of grazing on which the Common's vast species' diversity depends.

Daneway Banks SSSI (GWT) represents a further example of unimproved limestone grassland, featuring fly and green-winged orchids. Other important GWT Cotswold wildflower sites include Greystones Farm Nature Reserve (SSSI) near Bourton-on-the-Water, which has the southern marsh and early marsh orchids, while thirteen different kinds of orchid occur at the Elliott (Swifts Hill) Nature Reserve (SSSI), near Slad. Meanwhile, the Pasqueflower Reserve near

Cirencester is home to the largest British population of this beautiful, briefly flowering purple plant.

Other grassland sites can be found at Painswick Beacon, Brown's Folly, Stinchcombe Hill, Crickley Hill and Barrow Wake.

The nationally scarce Bath asparagus is a feature of the Bath and North East Somerset area, including parts of the Avon Wildlife Trust's Brown's Folly reserve. Also known as the Spiked Star of Bethlehem, it is thought the local presence of this pretty white and green star-shaped plant might be linked to the Roman occupation. Despite old records of the plant being sold at Bath market as an alternative, it is not related to the vegetable although it does resemble it at pre-flowering stage.

Minchinhampton and Rodborough Commons are owned and managed by the National Trust. Protected by law, the Commons (which jointly cover approximately 335 hectares) are nationally important for their history and wildlife, including at least eleven different types of orchid (among them the bee, pyramidal and early-purple), the juniper (a shrub found abundantly on Rodborough Common but rare within the rest of the Cotswolds), and the beautiful pasque flower, found on only a handful of sites in the Cotswolds.

This Common land is also seasonally grazed, continuing the ancient farming tradition. Local graziers turn out between 400 and 600 cattle every 13 May on Marking Day, their laid-back charm perhaps occasionally raising the blood pressure of some of the Commons' more time-conscious users – not that Dozy Daisy and her friends seem that concerned.

The rare limestone woundwort plant is protected at a SSSI near Wotton-under-Edge and is only found at one other site in Britain.

Cotswold pennycress (*Thlaspi perfoliatum*) is classified in Britain as 'vulnerable'. Ten out of the fourteen national sites for Cotswold pennycress are in the Cotswolds.

The Cotswolds is one of only two sites in Britain where the round-leaved feather-moss is found. It also has one of the largest British populations of the rare meadow clary.

The snowdrop clone *Galanthus elwesii* 'cassaba' was introduced from a collection made in Cassaba, Turkey, at the end of the eighteenth century. Despite the clone being thought no longer in cultivation, a form of cassaba was found in about 1990 in private woods near the Cotswold village of Daglingworth by renowned galanthophile, the late Ruth Birchall of Duntisbourne Abbots, who named and distributed it to other collectors. From there, the cassaba 'Daglingworth' made its way into the trade.

COTSWOLD PRESERVES – SIX BLUE BELLES, THREE RARE BEETLES AND THREE IMPORTANT SNAILS

The Cotswolds is nationally significant for the small blue butterfly and is part of the reintroduction programme for the large blue in the Stroud Valleys. The chalkhill blue, common blue and woodland-edge holly blue butterflies can also be found in the Cotswolds, as well as the adonis blue (back after thirty years).

The Cotswolds is an important stronghold for the rare Duke of Burgundy butterfly, and the marsh fritillary is seen around the Stroud area.

A tiny leaf beetle with a big name – *Cryptocephalus primarius* – is found on just two UK sites, both of them near Dursley.

One of the three UK sites for the violet click beetle is within the Cotswolds AONB and the rare bark beetle *Gastrallus imarginatus* has been found on a number of north Cotswold sites.

The only UK population of the endangered species of snail *Lauria Sempronii* makes its home on two stretches of dry stone wall at Edgeworth, while ancient Cotswold woodlands such as Frith Wood (GWT) are strongholds for the rare Bulin snail *Ena montana*.

Descendants of the so-called 'Roman snail' *Helix pomatia* can still be found in parts of the Cotswolds today, although, the species is generally so rare, it now has protected status. These creamy-coloured mollusc monsters are thought to have been introduced by the Romans who, before gobbling them up, reputedly fed them on milk until they were so obese they couldn't squeeze back in their shells.

COTSWOLDS ON THE WING

A report for the CCB by the RSPB in 2002 recorded eighty-six species of bird in the Cotswolds AONB, twenty of them occurring in nationally important numbers, including:

Dunnock
Goldfinch
Greenfinch
House Sparrow
Jackdaw

Linnet
Skylark
Starling
Whitethroat
Woodpigeon
Yellow Hammer

Ten per cent of the country's breeding horseshoe bats are found in the Cotswolds – particular strongholds for the lesser and greater horseshoe bat occur around Bath, Bradford-on-Avon, north-east of Cirencester and the former limestone quarries around Minchinhampton. At least twelve species of bat are found at Brown's Folly near Bath (Avon Wildlife Trust), including the rare greater horseshoe bat. One of their number, the so-called 'legendary boris', is rarer still. Last seen in January 2000, twenty-eight years after he was first ringed, this furry phenomenon laid claim to being the second oldest recorded bat in the world.

LEGBARS, KHAKIS & BROWNS – THREE EGGS-TRAORDINARY DOMESTIC BIRDS

Eau-de-nil, turquoise, celadon, sky blue and pink – the Cotswold legbar hen lays pastel coloured eggs which are sold all over the country. The hen was developed by breeder Philip Lee-Woolf at Winchcombe and descends from an old Cambridge University breed called the cream legbar, created by Professor R. Punnet in the 1940s using the offspring of three birds brought home by explorer and botanist Clarence Elliot to Stow-on-the-Wold from South America.

The Burford brown hen was originally developed by Mabel Pearman, whose husband, Tom, farmed at Westhall Hill in Burford during and after the First World War. Its thick-shelled, heavy, brown-coloured eggs are now sold nationwide.

The khaki campbell duck, notable for its superior egg-laying capabilities, was bred by Mrs Adele Campbell at Uley. An article from the *Evesham Journal & Four Shires Advertiser* of 1929 reports a khaki campbell duck laying 328 eggs during a 336 day test – such 'splendid records' (despite a drought) 'conclusively proving', it argues, 'the economic value of khaki-campbell ducks as food producers.' According to the article, the breed 'deserved to be cultivated on every farm or country estate.'

THE MAGNIFICENT COTSWOLD LION

But Cotswold men may sleep o' nights while Chancellor sits on wool,
Ten centuries of Cotswold sheep have kept their coffers full,
And sheep of lineage like ours maintain a due decorum,
Munching the languid years away in saecla saeculorum.

(*The Bertie Ramsbottom Book of Improbable Sheep*, Ralph Windle)

In terms of Cotswold mammals, there's only one clear winner – the noble 'Cotswold Lion', so dubbed due to its large frame and lustrous curly fleece.

Thought perhaps to have descended from the flocks of Roman times, Cotswold longwool sheep once covered the region's vast open hillsides, bringing, as their legacy of handsome 'wool churches' amply testifies, great power and wealth to the medieval merchants of the day via the export of the animals' renowned 'Golden Fleece'. It was as a meat producer, however, that the Cotswold was best known during the nineteenth century – another important era for the breed with pedigree rams in huge demand the world over, widely used for crossbreeding.

Unfortunately, changes in agriculture, wool and meat requirements gradually spelt disaster for the Cotswold sheep, so that by the 1960s only about 200 remained, prompting the decision in 1966 to revive the Cotswold Sheep Society – originally founded in 1891. Thankfully, the Cotswold sheep is still around – it is now listed as a Minority Breed on the Rare Breed Survival Trust Watchlist and there are currently about 1,500 registered pedigree ewes in the UK, mainly kept by private breeders. The attributes of the Cotswold sheep are also appreciated across the Atlantic. At the turn of the last century, there were approximately 70,000 of them in the USA – and there are still more Cotswold sheep in America than in the UK today.

Most of the Cotswolds' clip (about 1–2 tons per year) is sent to the British Wool Marketing Board for use in various wool products, including carpets. Cotswold fleece is also sought after by traditional hand spinners. The society has two trademarks – Pedigree Cotswold Lamb (marketed to the retail hospitality and tourism sectors) and Cotswold Wool.

Given their superior pedigree (not to mention rakish good looks), it can hardly come as a surprise to know that several Cotswold sheep have made it to the big screen over the years, counting such films as *Joseph Andrews*, *The Madness of King George*, *Pride & Prejudice* and *Mill on the Floss* among their 'flock'-buster appearances.

HORSE-PLAY

The relationship between the Cotswolds and the horse cannot be underestimated. A number of major equestrian events take place in the Cotswolds – the Mitsubishi Motors Badminton Horse Trials, Fidelity Blenheim Palace International Horse Trials and the Festival of British Eventing held at Gatcombe Park, near Minchinhampton among them.

As might be expected with Cheltenham Racecourse at hand (the Cheltenham Festival is famous the world over), the Cotswolds has a strong horseracing community.

The Hollow Bottom pub at Guiting Power (so named due to being set in a hollow at the bottom of the village) is well known for its tip-top racing connections – among its many visitors, totesport Cheltenham Gold Cup winner, Imperial Commander (2010) and Grand National winners, Earth Summit (1998) and Bindaree (2002) – all trained by Cotswold-based Nigel Twiston-Davies.

The 2010 John Smith's Grand National winner, Don't Push It, was trained by Cotswold-based Jonjo O'Neill and ridden by A.P. McCoy OBE MBE, who went on to become the 2010 BBC Sports Personality of the Year – the first rider to win the award.

Point-to-point racing is popular and extremely competitive, with races held at Andoversford, Didmarton, Siddington and Paxford.

The Cotswolds has five main hunts:

Cotswold Hunt
Cotswold Vale Farmers Hunt
Duke of Beaufort's Hunt
North Cotswold Hunt
Vale of the White Horse Hunt (VWH)

MORE NOTABLE COTSWOLD ANIMALS

Denizens of the picturesque, but precariously hilly village of Chalford have appointed their own personal delivery boys – two delightfully strong and capable characters whose arresting charm and unmistakeable star quality have not gone unnoticed by the press. Having appeared on TV and in many of the national newspapers, one might imagine such stardom to have gone straight to Teddy's and Chester's sweet woolly heads – but no. These faithful donkeys continue to deliver the villagers' shopping from the local community shop every week, and remain two of Chalford's most popular residents.

The Cotswolds has its very own 1930s touring circus, including horses from all around the world – and a goose called Brian. Based near Bourton-on-the-Water, the animals and artistes of Giffords Circus fill many village greens with wonderment during the summer months.

Cotswold residents Belinda and Rudi live near the River Frome and are the latest in a long line of tame Asian small-clawed otters whose mission over the past thirty years has been to promote the importance of clean water. The first otter, Bee, was raised in 1980 and became known all over the world (her death in 1993 was reported in America and even attracted a royal telegram). Belinda (aged twelve and a half) has appeared on several television programmes and has met Sir David Attenborough and HRH The Prince of Wales. Along with Rudi (aged four and a half) she attends thirty to fifty events throughout the summer, and is raising money for her persecuted otter cousins overseas.

Unfortunately, the Cotswolds can't lay claim to the famous Gloucester Old Spot pig (which originated in the Berkeley Vale) although two Tamworth porkers from Malmesbury did cause a bit of a media squeal in 1998, thanks to their dramatic bid for freedom from a local abattoir. Having been on the run for about a fortnight, the 'Tamworth Two' were finally apprehended (the tricky boar, by two butchers from Nailsworth), following which they were eventually sent, courtesy of a national newspaper, to an animal centre where they lived happily ever after.

WILD BEASTS ON THE COTSWOLDS

A unique dinosaur specimen discovered on Minchinhampton Common in the Cotswolds is held at the Natural History Museum, London. The partial skull of a *Proceratosaurus bradleyi*, was originally described as *Megalosaurus bradleyi,* but was later recognised as sufficiently distinctive to merit a new name of its own. The specimen has recently been re-described in detail in the *Zoological Journal of the Linnean Society of London.*

Impressive displays of dinosaur bones and fossil collections found in the Cotswolds feature in several local museums, including at Stroud's Museum in the Park, where one of two stegosaur dorsal plates, apparently representing the oldest confirmed stegosaur specimen in the world, can be seen (the other is in the Natural History Museum, London). Both plates were found in a quarry near Stow-on-the-Wold in the 1930s. Internationally important Megalosaurus remains found at the same location are also on display at Stroud.

The Oxfordshire Museum at Woodstock has a display of giant fossilised footprints (discovered at Ardley Quarry) thought to be from the dinosaur species Megalosaurus, as well as a life-size sculpture of a megalosaur – the first dinosaur to be described scientifically following the discovery of part of a bone near Chipping Norton in the 1600s.

The significance of the dolphin to Tetbury has long been a mystery, although there are plenty of these mythical creatures about town. One romantic theory for their appearance on the town's coat of arms relates to a former lord of the manor, whose life was apparently saved by two dolphins wedging themselves in the hole of his damaged ship.

The village of Compton Abdale has been inhabited by a crocodile for over 150 years. Actually, this toothsome wonder is made of stone and doesn't have a body, but he does have a mighty jaw through which the spring waters of Compton Brook gush forth into the River Coln. The conduit was restored in 2007, replacing the original croc which was sculpted in the nineteenth century.

Those of a nervous disposition should avert their gaze when visiting All Saints', North Cerney. There's a strange 'leopard' depicted on one of the church's tower buttresses, accompanied just round the corner by a 'brayne-eating' Manticore.

Historian Samuel Rudder records that the manor of Lechlade, near Fairford, was once held by a Danish baron called Siward. According to legend, his grandmother, a Danish princess, was 'ravished by a bear' while walking in a forest. This bizarre coupling soon resulted in a little baby sporting bear ears. This 'son of a bear' went on to succeed his mother, eventually becoming the father of Siward, who arrived in England during the reign of King Edward the Confessor. Grrr.

Just how the former coaching inn The Bear of Rodborough Hotel got its name, has long been a matter of debate. The best story involves a local man by the name of Peter Lusty, who once had the misfortune of bumping into a bear on his way home from the establishment (then called The Highwayman). Naturally, poor Peter was severely chastised by his wife, who thought he was wearing his beer goggles upside down – an injustice he probably held against her for some time for, as it turned out, a performing bear had indeed escaped from its keeper in the vicinity. The animal was later re-captured using 'wire netting, rope, honey and snuff'. Two large bears can still be seen hanging around the premises today, but don't worry – they've already eaten.

A Cotswold beast (pet) named Crumpet (principal role – 'frightening females') is often known to cause trouble during the summer months, although at the time of writing he's on his way to perform at the Bürgerfest in Bavaria. The Gloucestershire Morris Men's former 'beast of disguise', Trumpet, is no longer at large and now resides at the Gloucester Folk Museum (not currently on display). Yet another member of the herd, 'Stroud', is only let out at Christmas, when he takes the floor along with the Gloucestershire Morris Mummers.

You've been warned.

2

STONED

Knaps, knobs, tumps...the ancient lumps and bumps of the region are both numerous and fascinating. The Cotswolds AONB has an impressive 400 Scheduled Ancient Monuments and over 17,000 archaeological sites from Mesolithic to modern.

FIVE TOP TUMP TAGS

Whitefield's Tump on Minchinhampton Common is named after the famous preacher George Whitefield (born in Gloucester in 1714) who preached there on more than one occasion. In a letter dated 29 March 1743, he stated he had preached to 'about twelve thousand on Hampton Common at what the people now call "Whitefield's Tump", because [he] preached there first.' In July 1739, he reported finding 'no fewer than 20,000' people gathered on 'horseback and foot' to hear him.

Human remains from the Jack Barrow at Duntisbourne Abbots were re-buried in the churchyard of St Peter, where the inscription on a massive ivy-clad stone, topped with a cross, reads (in capitals), 'These rough stones taken from the barrow [at] Jack Barrow Farm cover the human remains found therein when it was opened 1875.' One of the excavated male skulls can also be found displayed in the archaeology gallery at the Museum in the Park, Stroud.

Plucky visitors can actually get inside Hetty Pegler's Tump, although its dark recesses are not for the faint-hearted – many human remains have been found there over the years (please check accessibility before visiting, as at 2011 the chambers are closed pending repair). As for the lady herself, she remains something of a mystery. Some say Mr and Mrs P once owned the land, others that the barrow was a lovers' meeting place. Whatever the truth, Hetty's name is often on the lips in these parts – one Cotswold brewery has introduced a real ale in her honour,

while a local barn dance ceilidh band called 'Hetty Pegler's Tump' has been dancing to her tune since 1976. (The name Pegler also turns up at Donnington, where a twin-bowl round barrow is known as Pegler's Knob.)

Another Cotswold lady is linked with a round barrow near Didmarton. Nan Tow's Tump is said to have been named after a local witch buried upright inside.

Eccentric Molly Dreamer from Minchinhampton doesn't have a barrow named in her memory, although she probably deserves one for effort. Apparently, she spent a great deal of her time in the nineteenth century digging for barrow treasure. No one knows for sure if her dream actually came true.

NOTABLE BIG 'UNS

The Long Stone near Minchinhampton is over 7ft high – its weathered, pockmarked surface clearly no turn-off for our ancestors, who apparently believed that passing a sickly baby through one of the holes in this enormous lump of oolite would effect a cure. If the holes remaining today are anything to go by, this dodgy remedy could only possibly have applied to exceedingly small babies.

The Hangman's Stone near Northleach gets its name from the sheep rustler who either fell over or sat down to rest on it – at which point the woolly wriggler tied round his shoulders unwittingly saved the hangman a job.

'Seven long strides shalt thou take, If Long Compton thou canst see, King of England thou shalt be.' Such was the prediction of some old hag that some old pretender to the throne had the misfortune to bump into at the Rollrights in Oxfordshire. According to legend, just as the poor chap took his seventh stride, the earth rose up and blocked his view of the village whereupon the wicked witch declared:

As Long Compton thou canst not see
King of England thou shalt not be...

...before turning him and all his men into great lumps of rock – hence the circle of 'King's Men' and five 'Whispering Knights' which make up the famous 'Rollright Stones'. Just across the way stands the 8ft -tall 'King Stone'.

The Whistlestone or Whittlestone (originally part of a nearby long barrow) can be seen outside the village hall at Lower Swell. It's said to

trot off to the Lady-well for a drink when it hears the clock at Stow-on-the-Wold strike twelve.

An old stone in Randwick Wood is known as the Lousey Stone as it apparently used to be the best place for the nit-gnawed to have a good scratch. Meanwhile, it's said you will get a nice warm feeling by merely standing next to the 6ft Tingle Stone near Avening.

THE ICONIC COTSWOLD DRY STONE WALL

The Cotswolds' pretty towns and chocolate-box villages are famous the world over – their distinctive architecture and beautiful 'honey-coloured' stone the subject of countless tourist guides and trails. No less handsome in its own sturdy way, the iconic Cotswold stone wall is also a key characteristic of the landscape.

The craft of dry stone walling has been practised in Britain for centuries – the earliest known example of dry stone walling in the Cotswolds being found at the famous Belas Knap long barrow, near Sudeley.

The vast majority of dry stone walls we see today, however, date from the eighteenth and early nineteenth centuries when large tracts of open land were enclosed.

There are approximately 4,000 miles of dry stone wall in the region – that's 6,437,376 metres. It takes about 1 tonne of stone to build a metre of Cotswold dry stone wall and a competent dry stone waller will build approximately 2 to 3 metres of 'standard' field dry stone wall in a day.

As much as of 60 per cent of the area's dry stone walls are currently either derelict or not stock proof.

Compared with days gone by, there aren't that many dry stone wallers in the Cotswolds today, although several courses and events are run by interested organisations each year in an attempt to redress this situation, including the CCB Open Dry Stone Walling Competition staged annually in partnership with the Cotswolds branch of the Dry Stone Walling Association of Great Britain. At the time of writing, approximately 1,200 folk of all ages and from all walks of life have received training from the CCB alone.

Building begins with the preparation of a shallow trench on which large, weight-bearing 'base' or 'foundation' stones are laid and then pinned using wedge-shaped pieces to prevent movement. The main body of the wall consists of two skins of coursed stones filled with carefully placed smaller hearting stones interspersed at approximately half-height with large 'throughs' which connect one face with another, so providing strength and stability. A typical field wall is 24in wide at the base and 15in under the cope. The wall tapers inwards from the base (called a batter) and each stone is tilted slightly downwards and outwards for drainage. At the required height (36in) the craftsman places a 'coping' – typically a row of irregularly shaped 'toppers' – on end along the top of the wall to give weight, stability and protection.

HOME SWEET HOME

The unique construction method of a dry stone wall, relying simply on its own weight and the craftsman's skill in choosing and fitting the right stones together, results in a structure of great strength which takes no goodness from the soil, doesn't require the maintenance of a fence, and has notable longevity. It's said that a well-built dry stone wall can stand for 200 years or more.

Apart from enclosing livestock and marking division of land, dry stone walls provide a vitally important habitat for many forms of wildlife including:

Adders

Bats

Bees

Blue tits

Coal tits

Cranesbill

Fieldmice

Grass snakes

Hedgehogs
Little Owls
Lizards
Millipedes
Moss
Pennywort
Polypody Fern
Redstarts
Robins
Shrews
Slow worms
Snails
Spiders
Spleenwort
Stoats
Stone chat
Stonecrop
Toads
Voles
Wall rue
Wasps
Weasles
Wheatears
Woodlice
Wrens

OFF THE WALL

It's not unusual for today's craftsmen to find items left behind by the dry stone wallers of the past including:

Animal bones
Bottles
Broken tools
Old coins – sometimes placed in the quoin (corner) of a wall
Medicine bottles
Snuff tins

The discoveries of an old bicycle holed up in the middle of a wide wall in Tetbury, two intact staddle stone bases (originally used as supporting bases for keeping, for example, granaries above ground), and a musket ball found in a wall at Lansdown, near Bath, are not representative.

BETWEEN THESE FOUR WALLS

The Stowell Park Estate near Northleach has 60–70 miles of dry stone wall. A particularly fine example runs along the Fosse Way between Fossebridge and Northleach.

At the time of writing, Cheltenham Borough Council is engaged in a grant-funded project to construct a 1,300-metre stretch of dry stone wall along the historic boundary of Cheltenham Borough and Cotswold District. The council's intention is for the wall to become part of the extensive grazing boundary surrounding Charlton Kings Common, which is also an SSSI. The site will be grazed by Dexter cattle that have been bred and raised on the Common. The long-term objective is to completely enclose the Common with a dry stone wall – approximately 3 miles long.

In 2010, approximately seventy 16-metre-wide sections of dry stone wall between Sapperton (near Cirencester) and Wormington (near Evesham) were dismantled and rebuilt by local craftsman, re-using original or locally sourced stone, during the installation of a new 28-mile underground gas pipeline installed by the National Grid.

A plaque set in the wall of the graveyard at Northleach unusually gives the name of the craftsman who laid it, but generally the craftsmen of the past remain anonymous. A beautiful carving of a Cotswold stone wall can be seen on the grave of a farmer in the churchyard of St Laurence's at Wyck Rissington and Cotswold stone walls feature in a fine stained-glass window illustrating the four seasons at St Bartholomew's, Notgrove.

DEWPONDS, SHEEP WASHES AND TURES

The faire and goodly flock, the shepheards onely pride,
As white as winters snowe, when from the rivers side
He drives his new-washt sheepe

Drayton

A Local Heritage Project called Wash Pool, undertaken in 2001, identified 148 sheep wash or wash pool sites across the Cotswolds AONB, including thirty-six found intact. Such stone-built structures were used up to the early twentieth century to wash sheep prior to shearing, thus increasing the amount the farmer could expect to get for the fleece. Good examples are found at:

Aldsworth
Ascott-under-Wychwood
Cleeve Common
Cutsdean
Farmington
Horsley
Kingham
Milton-under-Wychwood
Sutton-under-Brailes
Warmington, Warwickshire

Several old dewponds also remain in the Cotswolds. These clay-lined pits were built to capture rain and ground off-run, thus providing grazing stock in outlying pasture access to drinking water. Although there are thought to be many more, known examples include:

Cleeve Common – restored
Cotswold Farm Park – largely covered
Crickley Hill Country Park – restored
Ebworth – partially uncovered
Macaroni Downs between Eastleach and Aldsworth – two uncovered
Sevenhampton – restored
Stanway – thirty-one identified, two restored
Westonbirt – uncovered

Access to dewponds was sometimes provided by 'tures'. Constructed with dry stone walling, these peninsular extensions (up to 100 yards long and 10 yards wide) to the fields provided an original and energy-efficient way of enabling livestock to reach a water source. So far, seventeen of these rare features have been discovered in the Stanway area – Cutsdean (ten), Stanway (five), Pinnock (one) and Snowshill (one). Grant aid has enabled five (Jubilee, Old Hill, Kitehill, Durhams and Oldborough) to be restored in recent years.

3

BUILT TO LAST

LOOK UP – LANDMARKS, CHIMNEYS & BUSTS

Tyndale Monument
The impressive Tyndale Monument on Nibley Knoll, North Nibley, rises 111ft and was erected in remembrance of William Tyndale, 'translator of the English Bible who first caused the New Testament to be printed in the mother tongue of his countrymen', over 300 years after this local martyr was strangled and burnt at the stake in Flanders on 6 October 1536.

Fascinating memorabilia relating to the monument can be seen at the excellent Wotton-under-Edge Heritage Centre, and the martyr features in a strikingly vibrant stained-glass window at St Adeline's, Little Sodbury, where a notice outside states that the church was 'built in 1859 from the stones and plan of William Tyndall's [sic] little chapel behind Little Sodbury Manor.'

Beckford's Tower
Situated atop Lansdown Hill near Bath, the grand 120ft Lansdown or Beckford's Tower was originally built in 1827 for writer and patron of the arts William Beckford (died in 1844) to house his art and literary collections. The tower is now owned by the Bath Preservation Trust and is home to a Beckford-related museum collection.

Broadway Tower
Situated at 1,024ft above sea level, Broadway Tower – a dramatic folly built for the 6th Earl of Coventry on Broadway Hill at the end of the eighteenth century – marks the second highest point in the Cotswolds after Cleeve Cloud. Its open-mouthed gargoyles speak volumes about the tower's jaw-dropping views. Weather permitting, you can apparently spot up to fourteen counties from the top.

Devil's Chimney

Quarry workers' joke or satan's flue? This craggy outcrop sits high above the spa town of Cheltenham from whence, it is said, the evil one used to amuse himself by lobbing rocks down at the faithful on their way to church. The saints got the last laugh though, as the stones somehow returned to bury him underground before piling in on top to seal the deal. Some believe bored quarry workers from the former nearby Leckhampton Quarry created the 'chimney', and another theory simply points to natural erosion. A similar tale surrounds the legend-laden Meon Hill, near Mickleton, where one story goes that the same fellow aimed a missile at Evesham Abbey – and missed – hence the hill.

Other Edifices

The Somerset Monument, near Hawkesbury Upton, stands at approximately 100ft and was erected in 1846 'to the memory of General Lord Robert Somerset' (died in 1842) who served at the Battle of Waterloo in 1815.

Radway Tower, an octagonal tower on top of Edgehill, near Banbury, was built to commemorate the centenary of the first major battle of the Civil War, which took place at Edgehill on 23 October 1642.

The chimney of Bliss Mill on the outskirts of Chipping Norton is difficult to miss. This former Victorian tweed mill (now private apartments) was built by businessman and philanthropist William Bliss. His original factory suffered a devastating fire on Valentine's Day in 1872, costing some £65,000.

Other mighty mill chimneys still around with nothing to do but silently testify to the industrial hey-day of many a Cotswold valley include:

Dunkirk Mill, Nailsworth
Ebley Mill, Stroud
Ham Mill, Thrupp
Holcombe Mill, Nailsworth
Lightpill Mill, Rodborough

Longford's Mill, Nailsworth
New Stanley Mill, King's Stanley
Slaughter Mill (corn), Lower Slaughter
Stafford Mill, Thrupp
St Mary's Mill, Chalford
Woodchester Mill, Woodchester

MORE TO SEE

The 60ft (approximately) statue of Queen Anne at Cirencester Park was erected by the first Earl Bathurst in 1741 (whom she had created Baron Bathurst in 1711).

You don't need specs to spot Nailsworth's giant dangling kettle. Inscribed at its base with the words, 'MY JUBILEE 1887', this 82-gallon whopper copper was erected over the shop of a marketing-conscious grocer, trading from a shop in George Street (now an optician's) in the late 1800s. Once sporting the words 'Mazawattee Tea' in gilt letters, the kettle is thought to have been purchased from either Marlborough or Malmesbury – one local source reporting that it was actually filled with water and boiled over a tripod before being installed. Check out the second (life-size) kettle on the lid. There's also a similar, much smaller receptacle in Long Street, Wotton-under-Edge.

'The Prophet' statue which stands in The Avenue, Cirencester, was created by distinguished Viennese sculptor Willi Soukop RA (died in 1995). Another of Soukop's works, called 'Meditation', appears in the Skillicorne Garden behind Cheltenham Town Hall (unfortunately, not open to the public though the sculpture can be seen through a gate in the neighbouring Imperial Gardens).

EIGHT HANDSOME COTSWOLD HALLS

St Edward's Hall at Stow-on-the-Wold (erected 1877–8 at a cost of over £4,000) was funded by money (and subsequent interest) left unclaimed in the town's Provident Bank. Two houses were demolished in the Square to make room for it. A statue of St Edward can be seen over the door.

Two more houses were demolished to accommodate the Victoria Hall at Bourton-on-the-Water, built by public subscription to commemorate that monarch's Diamond Jubilee (June 1897). The building, which overlooks the pretty River Windrush, opened on 3 December 1898.

The beautiful Redesdale Hall at Moreton-in-Marsh sports a weathervane in the shape of a boar's head gripped by a pair of hands, representing part of the Mitford family crest. A plaque on the building records that it was erected in 1887 by Lord of the Manor of Moreton-in-Marsh, Sir Algernon Bertram Freeman Mitford CCVO KCB, 1st Baron Redesdale, in memory of the Earl of Redesdale who had died the previous year.

Nailsworth Town Hall began life as a Baptist 'Tabernacle' erected in 1867, when approximately sixty members of the nearby Shortwood Chapel went off and built their own church following a difference of opinion regarding the appointment of a new pastor.

The famous eighteenth-century actress Mrs (Sarah) Siddons (born in 1755) had several links with the Cotswolds, including the village of Minchinhampton near Stroud, which traditionally lays claim to an appearance by the legendary lady at its beautiful seventeenth-century Market House. Bewigged with ringlets and dressed in a blue striped gown, Mrs S now oversees the indoor weekly Country Market trapped inside a picture frame.

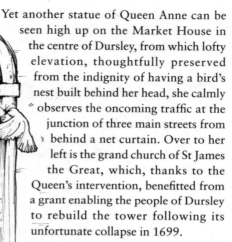

Yet another statue of Queen Anne can be seen high up on the Market House in the centre of Dursley, from which lofty elevation, thoughtfully preserved from the indignity of having a bird's nest built behind her head, she calmly observes the oncoming traffic at the junction of three main streets from behind a net curtain. Over to her left is the grand church of St James the Great, which, thanks to the Queen's intervention, benefitted from a grant enabling the people of Dursley to rebuild the tower following its unfortunate collapse in 1699.

Tetbury's stunning pillared Market House dates from 1655 (later altered and enlarged) and was originally used for wool stapling. The building has a weather vane consisting of two dolphins as well as two handsome clock faces – apparently the source of some irritation for the Revd Mr Alfred Theophilus Lee. Writing in 1857, he bemoans the fact that the town and church clocks were apparently at 'perpetual variance'. The church's clock and chiming mechanism were replaced in 1893 by Gillett & Johnston of Croydon (still in business) for £115 (clock) and £85 (chiming mechanism) – paid for by Hamilton Yatman of Highgrove House, now the country residence of HRH The Prince of Wales.

Stroud's imposing Subscription Rooms opened with a double concert in 1834. It is unlikely that Woodchester farmer William Radcliff was among the distinguished audience at either performance. He'd already starred in a pretty entertaining show of his own – an occasion which, to this day, remains one of Stroud's most well-known and famous stories. A report in the *Gloucester Journal* states that Radcliff had been to Tetbury Fair, where he'd imbibed 'quantum suff of liquor'. Having found the Swan in Stroud shut, the farmer then proceeded on horseback down a private road, where he found himself negotiating the scaffolding of the Sub Room building works, rashly declaring if he could not go under, he would go over! His obedient horse (worth £50) then proceeded to the extremity of the scaffolding before Radcliff became 'aware of his perilous situation', at which point, despite desperate attempts to put the poor animal into reverse, disaster ensued. Radcliff hastily caught hold of the bridle, in consequence of which the horse, 'precipitated from a height of nearly 30 feet', was 'dashed to atoms'. At least William had the distinction of a ramp being (unofficially) named in his honour. According to Stroud historian Paul Hawkins Fisher, the scaffolding was thereafter dubbed 'Radcliff Highway'.

AT LEAST 100 MORE INTERESTING PLAQUES & WHERE TO FIND THEM

A tablet erected by the Committee of the Village Itinerancy commemorating the ministry of the Revd Mr Rowland Hill AM (died in 1833), who 'exercised in almost every part of this kingdom for more than sixty years', still hangs on the wall of his former Tabernacle church (now an auction room) at Wotton-under-Edge. Mrs Hill, who died in 1830, gets a brief mention at the end. The precise whereabouts of her burial place had always proved difficult to establish – a mystery gruesomely solved when the church floor was raised during restoration a few years ago.

A plaque set on to a stone at Broadway Hill commemorates the names of five servicemen who lost their lives as a result of a crash there while on operational training in an A.W. Whitley bomber (Z6639) on 2 June 1943.

Another important memorial at Down Ampney records the fact that 'Douglas Dakotas from 48 and 271 Squadrons RAF Transport Command carried the 1st and 6th Airborne Divisions, units of the Air Despatch Regiment and Horsa gliders flown by the glider pilots regiment to Normandy-Arnhem and on the crossing the Rhine operations...' from the former airfield there in 1944–5. A service is held by the RAF Down Ampney Association each September at All Saints' Church, followed (subject to availability) by a solitary vintage aircraft flypast at the airfield, in tribute to Flight Lieutenant David Samuel Anthony Lord who was posthumously awarded the only VC for RAF Transport Command. Standing at this special windswept spot, as the sound of a solitary trumpet echoes across the Cotswold fields, is a profoundly moving experience. A garden of remembrance is situated at All Saints' churchyard while inside, a stained-glass window features the vibrant image of a Dakota aeroplane.

Thanks perhaps to Cupid, a hydrogen balloon flight made in 1784 by Edward Jenner (famous for pioneering a vaccine against smallpox) happened to touch down near the home of a certain Catharine Kingscote of Kingscote Park. A plaque in the porch of St John the Baptist, Kingscote records their subsequent union in 1788 stating, 'his marriage brought him much happiness'.

A plaque on a cottage opposite The Black Prince at Woodstock commemorates the raising of the first 'Blenheim Orange' apple tree.

A board at St Eadburgha's, Ebrington, records the bequeath of the 'milk of ten good and sufficient milch kine to the poor' of the village from 'May 10th to Nov. 1st annually for ever.' According to the inscription underneath, the charge was redeemed in 1952.

A plaque inside the door at The Cross Hands Hotel, near Chipping Sodbury, commemorates the occasion in December 1981 that Her Majesty The Queen took refuge there during a blizzard.

Seven men from the Royal Canadian Air Force, Royal Air Force VR and Belgian army, who lost their lives in a Vickers Wellington aircraft at Staple Farm, Withington on 19 April 1943, are remembered by a stone plaque at St Michael & All Angels, Withington. Officially opened in 1990 by the late Air Marshal Sir Ivor Broom KCB CBE DSO DFC AFC, the Wellington Aviation Museum at Moreton-in-Marsh is dedicated to all those connected with wartime RAF Moreton-in-Marsh. There is also a stone memorial outside the main gate of the former airfield (now the site of a Fire Service College).

A fascinating toll board at Moreton-in-Marsh lists the charges levied 'on all market, fair and other days', including: 'For every Roundabout driven by pony 5's to 6's per day.' The stated charge 'For every Horse or other Beast drawing any Coach, Stage Coach, Post Chaise, Diligence, Van, Caravan, Sociable Berlin, Landau, Chariot, Vis-a-Vis Barouche, Phaenton, Chaise, Marine Calash, Curricle, Chair, Gig, Whiskey Hearse, Litter or other such Carriage', on another restored board on the former toll house at Butterrow (now a private residence), is a mere 3*d*.

A stone memorial at the church of St Andrew in the village of Coln Rogers commemorates the safe return of all their number (twenty-five men and one woman) serving during the First World War, ending with the heartfelt words, 'Thanks be to Thee O God'. Happily, the serving men (and women) of Little Sodbury and Upper Slaughter also all came home.

A memorial at St Michael & All Angels, Guiting Power, records that Captain Powell Snell of Guiting Grange raised the first troop of Gloucestershire Yeomanry at the Plough Hotel, Cheltenham, in July 1795. A green plaque can also be found at what is now the entrance to the Regent Arcade Shopping Centre in Cheltenham.

The Millennium Steps at Malmesbury feature a series of plaques denoting notable dates in the town's history, and a pottery plaque commemorates the birthplace, in 1588, of the philosopher and political theorist Thomas Hobbes, whose major treatise *Leviathan or The Matter, Forme and Power of a Common Wealth Ecclesiasticall and Civil* was published in 1651. Malmesbury's Thomas Hobbes Society was founded in 1969. Its associated annual festival, established in 2008, has since burgeoned into England's first 'Philosophytown'.

Cirencester has thirty-four blue oval wall plaques and twenty-three brass pavement and footpath waymarks commissioned by the town's Civic Society, whose members also provide scheduled guided tours of this historic town from May to September, and at other times by arrangement. Another historic Cotswold town, Tetbury, has fifteen black and gold wall plaques commissioned by the Tetbury Civic Society, complemented by their locally available walkabout guide. Again, Civic Society members give guided tours by arrangement. Bath has a city trail of sixty-six commemorative mural tablets plus thirteen architect's plaques. Stroud has a series of thirteen informative heritage boards and four plaques commissioned by Stroud Preservation Trust and the Institute of Physics – walk leaflets available. Nailsworth has a part town/part countryside walk marked by eight history boards created by the Stroudwater Textile Trust – also complemented by a leaflet.

PASSING TIME IN THE COTSWOLDS

Nailsworth's 30ft clock tower, erected in 1952, was designed especially to carry the sound of its quarter and hour chimes up to the surrounding hillsides. Its bells, which are mounted upside down approximately 7ft above the floor, are struck inside the sound bow using special hammers.

A clock dated 1648 can be seen on Moreton's curious old Curfew Tower along with a bell dated 1633 – last rung (twice daily) by Curfew Bell Ringer William Webb, who died in 1862. A portrait of this well turned-out chap dressed in scarlet breeches and a black top hat appears in the front of the book *A Short History of Moreton-in-Marsh* by the Revd Mr W.L. Warne, although the whereabouts of the original painting is sadly unknown. A notice at St Edward's, Stow-on-the-Wold, records the fact that successive members of the same family were responsible for winding the clock there over a course of 110 years up to 2006.

Two portraits of Queen Victoria (newly painted early in the 1990s) can be seen above the impressive Tolsey House clock at Wotton-under-Edge. The clock was erected to celebrate Her Majesty's Diamond Jubilee (1897), replacing an earlier seventeenth-century timepiece. It's debatable whether Her Majesty would have been amused by the four Union flags seen sprouting above her head.

An interesting 'Noon Day' stone stands in the churchyard of St Martin's, Horsley – a shadow of the west buttress of the church tower strikes it at mid-day (sunshine permitting, of course). The current stone was erected approximately twenty years ago after the (unmarked) original was knocked over by a lorry.

Another clock with Nailsworth connections has recently found its way back to Wales. The grandmother clock, originally presented to poet W.H. Davies 'by admiring fellow townsfolk of his native town of Newport, on 30 October 1930', was gifted by Davies' great nephew of Nailsworth in 2010 and is now housed at the Newport City Museum.

Stroud's former National School still sports its rare Jack Clock featuring the figure of a boy holding a club ready to strike a little bell on the hour although, when I saw him, he appeared to be literally on strike – unlike Stroud's restored 'railway time' clock, which is definitely in good working order. This reminder of the days when Stroud time ran behind London is now housed in the town's museum. A single time standard (GMT) for Britain was made law in 1880.

A handsome eight-day two-faced clock once graced the window of a former post office at Dursley, along with a notice proudly stating that it showed 'Greenwich Time'. Having been forgotten about for many years, the 15in clock, with white dial and black hands, has recently been restored and now lives at the town's fascinating Heritage Centre.

St John Baptist, Cirencester still has an hourglass – once used in churches to monitor the sermon length. The former hourglass of St Mary's, Bibury, is no longer around, although a memorial to former minister, Benjamin Wynnington, who died in 1673, remains. According to local historian Rudder, Mr Wynnington was known for turning the glass a second time, thus detaining his congregation for yet another hour, during which the eminently sensible Lord of the Manor would usually retire to 'smoak his pipe'.

SMALL & SWEET

The picturesque village of Bourton-on-the-Water was reproduced in Lilliputian form in the vegetable garden of the village's Old New Inn during the 1930s. Using stone from Farmington Quarries, the 1/9 scale model took three to four years to build and the attraction opened just in time for Bourton's celebration of the Coronation of King George VI in 1937.

A quaint little black and white building (dated 1428) in New Street at Painswick is reputedly the oldest building in England to house a post office, while a chemist shop in Burford High Street lays claim to being the oldest pharmacy in England, dating back to 1734.

Charfield and Stroud each have an 'anonymous' pillar-box. Manufactured by A. Handyside, the box outside Charfield post office has an unusual high aperture and dates from 1879–83. Anonymous post boxes are so called because they don't have a Royal Cipher (VR) or the words 'Post Office' – believed to be an oversight on boxes manufactured between 1879 and 1887. There's also a large anonymous wall box at Broadway. Two very early wall boxes (1857–59) still in use in the region can be found at Kencot (Oxon) and Tortworth, while Tetbury has a replica Penfold box (a hexagonal box originally produced during the period 1866–79) which, although it has the VR cipher, is actually a modern replica version.

A beautiful old dovecote at Naunton was saved from development in 1999. Completely restored in 2001, the Grade II* listed Ancient Monument has four gables and 1,175 nest holes, many of which have been 'occupied' under a special 'Sponsor a Nest Hole' scheme. A *Great Dovecote Book* has been established to record the building's journey from Lord of the Manor status symbol to community treasure, as well as the dedications of its ever-increasing circle of friends. Future plans include the restoration of a nearby stone pump house (built 1925) in order to reinstate a turbine, powered by the picturesque River Windrush which flows through the village.

The former weavers' cottages of Arlington Row at Bibury are probably one of the most admired sights in the Cotswolds, although they apparently weren't always as comfortable as they look now. Celebrated author, the late P.H. Newby, CBE (inaugural winner of the Booker Prize with his novel *Something To Answer For* in 1968) lived in one of the cottages for part of his childhood, reportedly remembering it as 'quite basic'.

ROAMING ABROAD – SOME BITS OF THE COTSWOLDS THAT AREN'T WHERE THEY STARTED OUT

It's no secret that our American friends adore the Cotswolds – Henry Ford apparently liked them so much, he wanted to take bits of them home – including the previously mentioned Arlington Row. He eventually settled for a cottage from Chedworth, which was carefully packed in boxes amounting to 475 tons and sent via a specially commissioned 67-wagon GWR train to Brentford, before being shipped across 'the pond' to be re-erected (1930) as part of The Henry Ford museum in Michigan – an incident that didn't go unnoticed by Parliament. A stone forge from Snowshill was also shipped to the United States.

Nailsworth's Shortwood Chapel was dismantled and re-built over the valley at Newmarket in 1881. An inscribed stone on the front of what is now Christ Church records that the foundation stone was laid by secretary of the Baptist Missionary Society, Edward Bean Underhill LLD – an apparently soggy occasion undertaken on 16 June accompanied by 'a continuous downpour'. A bottle was duly placed in a wall cavity for posterity (containing such items as a history of Shortwood and two newspapers) and the hymn 'This stone to thee in faith we lay', duly sung.

The Metropolitan Museum of Art, Fifth Avenue, New York, houses nine panels of stained glass from Temple Guiting. The other three (of an original twelve sections) can be seen at the village church, where a notice states that the Talbot family originally sold the nine panels to a London dealer for £5 in the early 1800s.

A curious stone bee shelter at Hartpury, near Newent began life some 19 miles away at Nailsworth, which is where it was re-discovered in 1957 behind the town's former police station and courthouse. When the site was developed in 1968, volunteers from the Gloucestershire Beekeeping Association arranged for the 25ft by 8ft structure to be sited at Hartpury College (then known as Gloucestershire College of Agriculture and Horticulture). Following a much-needed restoration, the bee shelter was moved once more to its final resting place among the graves at Hartpury churchyard in 2002 – an occasion marked by the presence of the Chief Constable of Gloucestershire and the Bishop of Tewkesbury (who blessed and dedicated the fascinating structure). Research undertaken at the time revealed that the Cotswold limestone shelter, formerly thought to have been medieval, was actually built at Nailsworth in the 1800s by quarryman Paul Tuffley, whose family firm once provided stone for interior work at the Houses of Parliament.

Thankfully, the famous Woodchester Roman mosaic from about AD 325 isn't going anywhere. Buried under the deserted graveyard of a former church, it hasn't been uncovered for nearly forty years, largely due to the huge amount of interest it generates. The last showing reportedly attracted many thousands of visitors and an earlier viewing in 1926 had to be extended to accommodate all those eager to see it, including archaeologists from China, Egypt, South Africa, Australia and New Zealand.

Following the 1970s event, brothers Bob and John Woodward from Wotton-under-Edge were inspired to construct a full-size replica of the mosaic. Comprising over 1.5 million tesserae (cube like tiles), the resulting 47ft by 47ft 'Orpheus Pavement' took the brothers approximately ten years to complete. Unlike the original, the mosaic has been about a bit since then, having been shown at Bristol, Bath, Stroud and the BBC *Blue Peter* studios, as well as at Prinknash Abbey, its home for the last few years. At the time of writing, the pavement appears to be off on its travels again. It was recently bought at auction by an anonymous bidder – destination unknown.

Quite why a bust of Disraeli should grace the portal of the Corner Cupboard Inn at Winchcombe, no one seems very sure. The closest I've got to an answer is that it was purloined from one of the local estates and put there as a joke. Answers on a postcard please...

4

COTSWOLD GLORY

To leave the Cotswolds without having paid homage to at least one of the region's famous 'wool' churches (e.g. Northleach, Fairford, Cirencester) would probably constitute a sin – these monuments to the success of the area's former wool trade are exquisite and not to be missed.

For those who care to seek them out, however, dozens more ecclesiastical wonders await sitting out the centuries in all their Cotswold glory, from ancient Saxon splendour to victorious Victorian zeal.

With so many to choose from, it's only possible to mention a few favourites here – the best way to discover them all, of course, is to explore for yourself (although access is not always guaranteed).

LARGE, SMALL, TALL

St John Baptist, Cirencester, is one of the largest parish churches in the Cotswolds. Its external length measures 180ft with a maximum internal width (including nave, aisles and Trinity Chapel) of 104ft. Impressively large village churches include: the spacious St Andrew's, Toddington, with its tall spire; St Mary's, Bibury; St Mary the Virgin, Shipton-under-Wychwood; and St Mary the Virgin, Kempsford.

Special little churches are not difficult to find in the Cotswolds. Divinely diminutive personal favourites include: St Michael's, Duntisbourne Rouse; St James', Clapton-on-the-Hill; St Mary's, Syde; St Faith's, Farmcote (beautiful views); St Oswald's, Widford; and St Leonard's, Lower Lemington.

At 198ft, the magnificent spire of St Mary Our Lady of Bloxham is visible for miles around, as is the spire of St Mary the Virgin and

St Mary Magdalen in Tetbury, which measures 186ft (to give some perspective, Nelson's Column is 169ft).

FIVE LEFT BEHIND

The atmospheric old church at Ampney St Mary stands in a field almost a mile from its former parishioners' 'new' home – some judiciously placed pots of ivy serving as reminders of the time the affectionately dubbed 'Ivy Church' was covered in the plant due to its once neglected state.

Broadway's beautiful St Eadburgha's Church is situated about a mile from the village. Its unusual dedication (also at Ebrington) relates to King Alfred's granddaughter, an abbess. (Incidentally, there's another church dedicated to St Alidhelm and St Eadburgha's in Broadway, Somerset).

The church of St Nicholas stands apart from the village of Oddington, which was re-built nearby in the eighteenth century, eventually leaving this captivating gem to a potentially lonely future – although perhaps not completely so. According to local tradition, a vixen and her cubs once occupied the pulpit. The same pulpit was also graced by the late Sir Michael Hordern, who delivered a most memorable 'sermon' during the filming of Henry Fielding's novel, *Joseph Andrews*, in 1977.

The thirteenth century church of St Oswald, Widford, stands on the site of a Roman villa along the beautiful Windrush valley. With its tracings of wall paintings and mosaic/pottery fragments, this peaceful and enchanting place is difficult to leave.

Marooned among the cornfields, surrounded by rolling Cotswold countryside, the special little church of St Arild's (Oldbury on the Hill) abides in perfect peace, a revolving iron gate ushering the unsuspecting visitor through shoulder-high cow parsley into a dreamlike scene perfectly frozen in time. Inside, its flagstoned, box-pewed glory sucks up time – the aching silence interrupted only by an occasional chatter of sparrows dust-bathing outside the porch.

St Arild's is cared for by The Churches Conservation Trust, as are the following churches in the region no longer needed for regular worship:

Gloucestershire (G), Wiltshire (W)

St John the Baptist, Inglesham (W)
St Michael & St Martin's, Eastleach Martin (G)
St Nicholas of Myra, Ozleworth (G)
St Mary's, Shipton Sollars (G)
All Saints', Shorncote (G)
St Saviour's, Tetbury (G)
St James', Charfield (G)

INSPIRING SPIRES & TOPPLING TOWERS

An ancient sculpture of Christ can be seen on the tower at St Mary's, Beverston, while a carved dog lives on the tower at St John the Baptist, Coln St Aldwyns.

The south doorway and western tower arch at St Nicholas of Myra, Ozleworth are remarkable examples of fine thirteenth century-carving and design. This Norman church also features a rare hexagonal tower and a circular graveyard.

The tower of St John the Baptist, Colerne sports a magnificent one-handed turret clock.

A detached tower stands in the grounds of Malmesbury Abbey while Holy Trinity in Minchinhampton has an unusual truncated spire topped with a corona. The spire of All Saints', Bisley is said to have been used as a landmark by German pilots during the Second World War.

St Mary's in Painswick and St Cyr's in Stinchcombe have defied the odds having both been struck by lightening twice. Gloucestershire bell expert Mary Bliss MBE tells the story of St Cyr's, struck once in 1883 (when the spire was toppled) and again in 1971, shortly after a spirited controversy regarding the proposed installation of an electrical chiming apparatus. The dilemma (which ended up at Consistory Court) was eventually solved by re-hanging the bells for full circle ringing and installing the chiming apparatus although, somewhat amusingly, only the electrical apparatus was put out of action as a result of the second strike, which happened on the very day of dedication. Meanwhile, St Mary's in Painswick was struck in 1765 (narrowly missing a chap winding the church clock) and again in June 1883, when some 40ft of the spire collapsed with parts crashing through the belfry and the roof of the nave, embedding the bells in debris. Re-building the spire on that occasion cost £1,498 18s 4d. The pinnacle can still be seen inside the church, where it serves as a rather nice occasional flowerpot.

Incidentally, it would clearly take more than a mere flash of lightning to scare the teddy bear fraternity of Painswick parish. Over one hundred of them have parachuted from St Mary's tower on at least two occasions in recent years in order to raise aid for charity. The brave bears are hoisted up in a bucket before being chucked over the edge (75ft from parapet to ground).

BIG BONG, LITTLE BONG

A 'ring' consists of a set of bells hung for ringing full circle. Most of the churches in the Cotswolds have between one and six bells, although St Mary's in Painswick has a ring of 13 + 1 and St John Baptist, Cirencester has a ring of 12 + 1.

St Bartholomew's, Winstone has the oldest bell in a ring of bells (i.e. rung full circle) in the Gloucestershire Cotswolds (dated *c.* 1320).

Christ Church in Chalford has the only ring of steel bells in the Cotswolds, cast in the mid-1800s at Sheffield.

Three of the bells at St Leonard's, Bledington, are inscribed with the names of kings – 'GOD SAVE KING WILLIAM' (fifth bell), 'GOD SAVE KING GEORGE' (third bell) and 'CHARLES HE IS OVR KING' (earthbound).

Many Cotswold church towers contain at least one bell cast by a member of the Rudhall dynasty – a famous Gloucestershire family of bell founders whose work in the county spanned from 1684 to 1835. St Nicholas in Lower Oddington has the first bell known to come from the Rudhall foundry (1684) – cast by the founder member, Abraham, whose memorial can be seen at Gloucester Cathedral.

The treble is the bell with the highest note in the set and is usually the lightest. The tenor bell has the lowest note in a set and almost always weighs the most. Its name comes from the Latin meaning 'to hold'. Some of the heaviest tenor bells in the Cotswolds are at St John Baptist, Cirencester (27cwt 1qr 16lb) and St Edward's, Stow-on-the-Wold (27cwt 2qr 24lb). The tenor at Bath Abbey weighs 33cwt 0qr 25lb and is the heaviest in Bath while St George's, Brailes (Warwickshire), has a tenor weighing 29cwt 0qr 19lb. Twenty cwt equals one ton.

A piece of continuous ringing consisting of at least 5,000 changes with no repeated changes is called a peal. It takes approximately 3 hrs 25 minutes to ring a peal at St John Baptist, Cirencester, where today's bell ringers still observe the old custom of ringing the 'Pancake Bell' at mid-day on Shrove Tuesday. A bequest to ring between 6.00 and 6.30 a.m. on 29 May each year, in commemoration of the Restoration of the Monarchy of 1660, is also faithfully maintained. Several other Cotswold churches still follow the tradition of ringing half-muffled on 31 December before taking the muffs off and ringing open to welcome in the New Year.

A delightful model at Avening's Church of the Holy Cross depicts the mischievous 'Rape of the Cherington Bell'. Late one winter's night in about 1830, St Nicholas' in Cherington was denuded of its tenor bell by some Avening folk keen to augment their own tower quota from five to six – perhaps confident in the belief of the day that it was quite alright to purloin a bell from one tower, just as long as you got it hung in another one without being caught. Evidently, not such a reliable maxim as the Avening thieves soon found themselves doing time. An amusing song of the day ends:

> Sorry we are for what we've done,
> We're paying dearly for our fun;
> Oh, that we were out of the cells,
> We'd ne'er again take Cherington bells.

FOUR TUNEFUL COTSWOLD BELL INSCRIPTIONS

Holy Cross, Owlpen (single bell):
'WHENE'ER THE SWEET CHURCH BELL/PEALS OVER HILL AND DELL, /MAY JESVS CHRIST BE PRAISED'

St Mary's, Painswick (third):
WHEN YOV ME RING I.LE SWEETLY SING 1731

St Laurence's, Stroud (treble):
IN SWEETEST SOUND LET EACH ITS NOTE REVEAL: MINE SHALL BE FIRST/TO LEAD THE DULCET PEAL

St Edward's, Stow-on-the-Wold (third):
WITH A MERRY NOTE NOW GOD PERMIT THAT I LONG TYME MY PLACE TO FITT/OCTOBER THE 16 ANNO 1620

ALL SAINTS

The most frequent church dedication in the Cotswolds is to St Mary. Other popular dedications include:

All Saints
St Andrew
St Bartholomew

St George
St James
St John
St Kenelm
St Lawrence
St Michael
St Nicholas
St Paul
St Peter

Less frequent occurrences include:

St Adeline – Little Sodbury
St Alban – Stroud
St Anne – Whelford
St Arild – Oldbury on the Hill
St Barnabas – Box, Snowshill
St Catherine – Westonbirt
St Cyr – Lacock (St Cyriac), Stinchcombe, Stonehouse
St David – Moreton-in-Marsh
St Eadburgha – Broadway, Ebrington
St Edward – Evenlode, Hawling, Stow-on-the-Wold
St Faith – Farmcote, Overbury
St Giles – Coberley, Hillesley, Uley
St Julian – Wellow
St Luke – Frampton Mansell
St Margaret – Bagendon
St Mary the Virgin and St Mary Magdalen – Tetbury (formally dedicated to both saints by the Bishop of Gloucester in 2006)
St Matthew – Cainscross, Coates
St Osmund – Tarlton
St Oswald – Compton Abdale, Shipton Oliffe, Widford
St Philip – Little Rollright
St Saviour – Tetbury
St Simon and St Jude – Milton-under-Wychwood
St Swithun – Leonard Stanley, Quenington, Bathford

The churches at Hailes, Tresham and Combe Hay appear saintless – their dedications are unknown.

The story of St Kenelm is as sad as it is unreliable. Kenelm (son of Kenulf, King of Mercia, who died in 821) supposedly ascended the throne at just seven years old, only to have his head hacked off (thanks to power-crazy sister Quendrid) in a Worcestershire wood frequented by a white cow. News of this shocking act miraculously reached the pope with the timely aid of a dove. After an unseemly tussle with the folk of Worcestershire, Kenelm's headless body was eventually brought to Winchcombe for burial. Apparently, quirky Quendrid then attempted to steal the limelight by singing the 109th Psalm, although it clearly wasn't up to much for she 'got buzzed off' at the twentieth verse and her eyeballs dropped out. As for Kenelm, he was duly canonised, his relics bringing the faithful flocking to Winchcombe for years to come, much to the satisfaction of the monks. The church of St Peter contains two stone coffins discovered on the site of the former abbey – one has an indentation for a head, the other doesn't.

Another little boy, in the form of a beautiful statue of the child St Cyr, can be seen on the church tower at Stinchcombe. According to legend, the infant Cyricus met his death having been thrown to the ground during his mother Julitta's trial for her faith in the reign of the Roman emperor, Diocletian.

St Lawrence's Well, opposite the old church at Didmarton, is said never to run dry following a blessing by the saint who succeeded Augustine (traditionally believed to have preached and performed a miracle at Long Compton) as Archbishop of Canterbury.

What little is known about local saint Arild (Oldbury on the Hill and Oldbury-on-Severn) does not make happy reading. She died at Kington (near Oldbury-on-Severn) defending her virginity from an odious tyrant called Muncius who, says historian Leland, 'cut off hir heade becawse she would not consent to lye with hym.'

A striking stone figure of St Agatha can be seen set in the wall of St Lawrence's, Lechlade – her breasts apparently pierced by a sword, indicating the sickening manner in which legend says she was tortured.

MORE BODY PARTS

There is a headless stone cadaver on one of the window sills of St James the Great in Dursley, and the stone head of an anonymous lady at St Mary the Virgin, Shipton-under-Wychwood, rests by her side. An ancient carving built into the wall of St Peter's at Ampney St Peter features a strange little 'Sheela-na-Gig' character bearing a huge head. There is also a replica of a rare twelfth-century carved 'head of Christ' (along with one of his feet) displayed at All Hallows', South Cerney.

A huge large-lipped beardy head (accompanied by all manner of boggly-eyed brethren) glares down from the parapet at St Barthlomew's, Aldsworth, and a head with two faces can be spotted on one of the tower corners at St Nicholas', Oddington. Meanwhile, the tympanum at St Andrew's, Great Rollright has a carved 'Jonah'-type fish, appearing to either gollop or regurgitate a human head.

The frightful company of grotesques glaring down from St Peter's in Winchcombe are supposed to have been modelled on some of the town's former residents – thankfully, today's locals are much better looking.

A stone demon gleefully chews on some poor chap's hand at St John the Baptist, Coln St Aldwyns, while St Michael's in Dowdeswell has an amazing brass of a priest in a processional cope – perhaps a memorial to a former abbot from Hayles Abbey, says Bigland. Whoever he was, he had incredibly long fingers.

It's a case of a missing person at St Peter's in Rendcomb, where the church's famous font features all the apostles except Judas.

There's a most unnerving 'eye' on John Beale's wall monument next to the organ at St Mary's in Temple Guiting, while an imp-like face lurks on a wooden screen at the back of St Peter's, Winchcombe. Another sinister visage (which appropriately disappears from view as you approach the altar) can be seen at the bottom of a glass panel at St John Baptist, Cirencester, and the startling face of the Green Man peers out of the sides of the fonts at Holy Rood, Daglingworth and St Mary the Virgin, Shipton-under-Wychwood.

The execrable grinner reclined at the feet of an angel at the church of St Mary Magdalene in Sherborne is short of a few metatarsals while, judging from a purely aesthetic point-of-view, the following monumental footwear simply cannot go unnoticed. One of the Whittington family figures at St Bartholomew's in Notgrove sports a pair of platforms 'to die for' while up above, his companion's feet are, frankly, enormous.

GLORIOUS GLASS

The famous stained-glass windows at St Mary the Virgin, Fairford, are, quite rightly, on every Cotswold visitor's must-see list. An outstanding twenty-five-year restoration project run by The Friends of Fairford Church, costing in the region of £500,000, was completed amid much rejoicing in 2010.

All Saints' in Selsley is renowned for its beautiful stained glass created by several Arts and Crafts luminaries.

A friendly looking St Bernard dog can be seen in a panel of glass at St Matthew's, Coates.

The story of a Cotswold herdsman suffering from leprosy features in six panels of stained glass at Canterbury Cathedral, one of which depicts the poor chap being passed food on the end of a long board in an effort to avoid infection. Things were so uncomfortable for young Richard Sunieve of Edgeworth that chroniclers report there was not 'the space of an arrow's point sound' on his ulcer-ridden body. Thankfully, however, he eventually made it to the sepulchre of St Thomas à Becket at Canterbury where, to cut a long story short, he drunk water from a well in the crypt mixed with a spot of the saint's blood and was miraculously healed. A figure of an archbishop can be seen in an ancient fragment of stained glass at St Mary's, Edgeworth.

Part of a pane of breathtakingly beautiful twentieth-century stained glass at St Mary's in Bibury was featured on the Royal Mail's first-class Christmas stamps in 1992. Dressed in a star-trimmed cloak, her bare feet touching a rainbow, the Virgin Mary is shown carrying the infant Jesus. The glass (designed by Karl Parsons) commemorates Rowland Cooper and his wife, who once lived at Bibury Court. A charming image of Mr Cooper's much treasured coach can be seen at the bottom.

A window at St Mary's in Swinbrook contains fragments of old glass rescued from a section of the church's east window, which was shattered when a German landmine with attached parachute exploded nearby at 9.20 p.m. on 26 September 1940. An inscription in the glass describes how the vicar of the day, William Grenville Boyd, collected and began arranging the pieces that now make up the window bearing his name.

HEAVENLY MUSIC

A plaque on the organ at St Laurence's in Wyck Rissington records that Gustav Holst (born in 1874) was organist there from 1892 to 1893. Volunteers of Cheltenham's Holst Birthplace Museum have recently devised a route called the 'Gustav Holst Way', featuring many locations associated with the famous composer. Designed to be undertaken from Cranham to Wyck Rissington via Cheltenham and Bourton-on-the-Water, the medium-distance historic walk (35 miles in all) is accompanied by a handy guide revealing such fascinating

Holst-related titbits as the rising star's Rissington remuneration – a down-to-earth £4 per annum.

Unlike Cheltenham, we can't boast a spa visit by George Frideric Handel, although apparently he may have played the handsome Shrider organ purchased in 1800 from St Martin-in-the-Fields, London, for the church of St Mary the Virgin in Wotton-under-Edge. Lettering on the case reads, 'The GIFT of His most Sacred MAJESTY, KING GEORGE. 1726'. Wotton's incumbent at the time was 'editor of psalmodies' William de Chair Tattersall, who was also chaplain to King George III from 1803.

No doubt, all of the above would have eagerly joined the queue of musical connoisseurs keen to sample the delights of the grand pipe organ at Cirencester's parish church. The 'Father' Henry Willis instrument was entirely re-built by the firm Harrison & Harrison during 2009 and is now considered to be one of the finest in the country. It has four manuals, sixty-three speaking stops, multiple pistons and playing aids with 128 general and eight divisional memory levels, and, very rare on English organs, a pedal divide. Henry Willis (who died in 1901) was the leading English organ builder of his generation, responsible for many famous organs including those in the Royal Albert Hall, London, and St George's Hall, Liverpool.

Two carved musicians can be seen on the tower of St John the Evangelist's at Elkstone – one playing the shawm (reed instrument), another, a cross-legged fellow, playing a citole (stringed instrument). A carved man clearly enjoying his own bagpipe playing greets you in the porch at St James the Elder at Horton.

More musical instruments can be found carved on the fourteenth-century font at St Peter and St Paul's, Northleach, which depicts angels playing a variety of ancient musical instruments including the rebec and psaltery. Another two musical angels swoon above eye level at St Peter's in Rendcomb.

A stone memorial at St Lawrence's, Lechlade, records that long-serving sexton Alfred George (born in 1853) was the church's organ-blower for sixty-three years.

A curious old stringed instrument described as the 'Crumbling Cello' can be seen encased at St Peter's in Winchcombe. It was originally played at the former Gretton Old Church not far away, whilst a picture of a strange looking 'Serpent' instrument, formerly played at St Mary the Virgin, can be seen at Shipton-under-Wychwood.

There are a number of tune-playing or chiming mechanisms in the Cotswolds including:

Bath Abbey

A chime-tune machine plays a different melody once through, each day of the week at 9 a.m., 1 p.m., 5 p.m. and 9 p.m., after the clock has struck. Hymn tunes at the time of writing are:

'The Church's one foundation' (with one note fudged) – Sunday
'The Church of God a kingdom is' – Monday
'Come ye faithful, raise the anthem' – Tuesday
'Alleluia! Sing to Jesus!' – Wednesday
'How sweet the name of Jesus sounds' (another with one note fudged) – Thursday
'From all that dwell below the skies' – Friday
'Teach me, my God and King' – Saturday

St George's, Brailes

'Jesus, where'er thy people meet' (Wareham) – 12 noon and midnight
'Lead, kindly Light, amid the encircling gloom' (*Lux benigna*) – 4 a.m. and 4 p.m.
'Come ye yourselves apart and rest awhile' (St Agnes) – 6 a.m. and 6 p.m.
'Abide with me; fast falls the eventide' (Eventide) – 9 a.m. and 9 p.m.
'Christ is gone up' (St David) – Sundays at each of the above times

St Michael's, Buckland

'We love the place, O God' – 8 a.m., 12 noon, 4 p.m. and 8 p.m.

St Lawrence's, Bourton-on-the-Water

The chimes sound every quarter and the following hymn tunes play, from 6 a.m. to 9 p.m., every three hours:

'We love the place, O God' – Sunday
'Christian, seek not yet repose' – Monday
'The sun is sinking fast' – Tuesday
'To the name that brings salvation' – Wednesday
'Christ is gone up' – Thursday
'Sweet the moments, rich in blessing' – Friday
'Days and moments quickly flying' – Saturday

St James', Chipping Campden

Tunes play 9 a.m., 12 noon, 3 p.m. and 6 p.m. These are:

'O worship the King'
'Holy Holy Holy'
'Belle Isle March'
'Blue Bells of Scotland'

St John Baptist, Cirencester

'O Faith of England' – 9 a.m., 12 noon, 3 p.m., and 6 p.m.

St James the Great, Dursley

Every three hours, starting at midnight:

'We love the place, O God' (*Quam delecta*) – Sunday
'God moves in a mysterious way' (London New) – Monday
'Thy way, not mine, O Lord' (Ibstone) – Tuesday
'Blest are the pure in heart' (Franconia) – Wednesday
'Songs of praise the angels sang' (Culbach) – Thursday
'Sweet the moments rich in blessing' (Batty) – Friday
'Through the night of doubt and sorrow' (St Oswald) – Saturday

St Peter and St Paul's, Northleach

'O worship the King, all glorious above' (Hanover) – day and night at
3, 6, 9, and 12, and chimes every quarter.

St Mary the Virgin and St Mary Magdalene, Tetbury

Metrical setting of Psalm 113 (tune: 'O Mensch, bewein') plays at
9 a.m., 12 noon, 3 p.m. and 6 p.m.

HOLY GRAFFITI

A soldier called Anthony Sedley painstakingly scraped his name on the lining of the font at St John the Baptist, Burford, in 1649, describing himself as 'Prisner'. Quite true, as unfortunately for him he was one of a large group of Levellers holed up in the church for several days at the mercy of Oliver Cromwell during the Civil War. A plaque outside commemorates three of his colleagues: Cornet Thompson, Corporal Perkins and Private Church, who were executed the morning of 17 May in the churchyard, in view of their comrades.

An inscription on one of the sills at St Michael's, Dowdeswell, states 'AO 1577/THIS SPIER WAS BVLT BY...' followed by a list of names, while a section of stone at St James', Clapton-on-the-Hill, is incised with a fascinating two-line 'indulgence'.

Stone window ledges at the Nailsworth Quaker Meeting House have initials and dates carved by school children in the late 1600s. The name Anthony Kingscote, followed by the date 1615, is carved into the screen at St John the Baptist, Kingscote, while at St Peter's in Rendcomb the name 'William Clevely' followed by the date 1707 is ornately scratched on the porch wall.

The tower of St Michael's in Duntisbourne Rouse bears the date 1587 along with an inscription of names, and the date 1461 appears in Arabic numerals on a buttress at St Andrew's, Chedworth, as well as two other inscriptions, '1485' and '1491', elsewhere.

A Greek palindrome graces the steps of the font at St John the Baptist, Coln St Aldwyns.

An incision on one of the pillars at St Mary's in Painswick improvises on Edmund Spenser's *The Faerie Queene*: 'Be bold, Be bold, but not to [sic] bold'. It is said to have been carved by one of the soldiers imprisoned in the church during the Civil War.

A PICTURE PAINTS A THOUSAND WORDS...

...which, in the case of medieval church wall paintings, is exactly what they were intended to do – such 'story' pictures being a common means of religious instruction for the mainly illiterate congregations of the day. Thankfully (although inevitably faded), several Cotswold churches still retain examples of such paintings, having somehow managed to survive the iconoclastic and 'restoration' horrors of the past. Space permits only a few entries here.

The vibrant red, brown and green wall painting at St Mary Magdalene, Baunton, shows a bearded St Christopher striding robustly among little fish as he carries the infant Jesus across the water. Medieval belief maintained that no one who looked upon the image of St Christopher (patron saint of travellers among other things) would suffer harm that day, hence his prominent position on many church walls.

A huntsman and three dogs gad across a wall at Hailes towards a pretty hare crouched under a tree. Other paintings include an enormous St Christopher, a wavy haired St Catherine, a slightly worse for wear St Margaret, not to mention an elephant with wings, a griffin, a basilisk and an owl.

An impressive and witty Last Judgement or Doom survives at St Nicholas', Oddington. Situated on the north wall, the picture shows the earth giving forth its dead to be judged, with an enthroned Christ at the top accompanied by his apostles and the faithful gathered round

about. Elsewhere the saints are welcomed in to the heavenly city (a curious brick affair) by angels – one fellow literally being hoisted to safety – while those not so fortunate are herded towards a welcoming party of ghastly looking, stripily-clad demons as a colleague busily fuels the fire with a pair of bellows in order to boil the poor, wretched sinners in a cauldron.

Parts of another historically important Doom (showing barefoot apostles, seated in pairs either side of the Virgin Mary) plus other fragmentary wall paintings remain at St Leonard's in Stowell – although if you can actually find Stowell first time, you are to be congratulated.

The delightful little church of St Michael's at Yanworth is home to a rather jolly looking skeleton – unfortunately, depicting Death (and somewhat fainter than this picture). Leaning nonchalantly on his spade, this suave fellow grins down from the wall, a handy shroud and scythe at the ready. Another Father Time type figure spans out the years at All Saints', Salperton, his surprisingly plumpish looking feet planted firmly on a black coffin.

The tiny church of All Saints', Shorthampton, has fascinating wall paintings featuring images (some fragmentary) including the Virgin Mary holding infants Jesus and St John with a bird, St Loy, St Zita, St Frideswide, and an exquisite solitary dragon's wing.

Bright red rose-type flower paintings (signifying the rosy cheek symptom of the plague) feature on the arches at All Saints' in Down Ampney.

The light, airy church of St Leonard's, Bledington, has several fragments of wall painting including a large Royal Arms and a crowned saint with doey eyes and bottom-length hair.

YOU MAY BE SEATED

Unusual stone bench ends feature at St Andrew's in Kingham, while the distinctive original box pews (tall enough to facilitate the occasional power nap with ease) at St Mary the Virgin and St Mary Magdalen, Tetbury are well worth trying out.

St Lawrence's in Didmarton has charming, high-backed (and exceedingly narrow), spearmint green pews and a triple-decker pulpit (pulpit, minister's pew and clerk's desk) with sounding board. Better keep your beanie on here, though, for the hat pegs are located up in the eaves (there used to be a gallery).

Presumably, the vicar of the day was not in any hurry to remonstrate with the perpetrators of several deep ridges etched into the stone seats of the porch at St Nicholas', Lower Oddington. These are thought to have been made by archers sharpening their arrows.

Lack of attendance at church (due to their lonely profession) is said to have prompted shepherds to take the precaution of leaving a mark of their trade in their coffins – i.e. a piece of wool. The shepherds of Stanton, however, appear to have been less willing to take the risk, as several dog tether grooves can be seen on the ends of some of the benches at St Michael & All Angels. There are also some fascinating old 'shepherds' pews' at St Michael's in Buckland.

Things are a little more strict at St Mary's in Hawkesbury Upton, where a half-moon shaped notice states, 'It is Desired That all Persons that come to this Church would be Careful to leave their Dogs at home & that the Women would not walk in with their Pattens on.'

5

COTSWOLD CRIMES

GUMSTOOLS, STOCKS & LOCKUPS

Several examples of stocks can be found in the Cotswolds today including a magnificent seven-holer outside the town hall at Winchcombe (the locals will tell you Winchcombe once had a one-legged rogue), and a five-holer at Woodstock (presumably they also had a hobbledehoy). A two-holed version can be found in The Square at Stow-on-the-Wold, a replacement four holer (plus whipping post) has recently been installed at Ozleworth and there's a set of iron stocks situated near the parish church at Painswick. Once found in practically every town or village, the stocks were widely used in the punishment of minor offences for both men and women. Typically consisting of two wooden boards fixed around a combination of neck and hands or feet (neck and hands only on a pillory), the perpetrator could expect anything from mere humiliation to expiration from exposure, as well as being pelted with whatever detritus the local population saw fit to propel. Indeed, one such miserable wretch is reported to have died from injuries suffered while in the stocks at Stroud in October 1832.

Judging by this announcement (*Stroud Free Press*) in the early 1850s, it appears the Painswick stocks were deemed particularly necessary:

> We have to make the ominous announcement that a pair of stocks have been erected for the punishment of those who carry on their carousals to the annoyance of their more sober neighbours. The late unwanted hilarity which has called for their erection has been attributed by the parties concerned to the purity of the air, but although we have heard a good deal lately about the virtues of "the wind", we are inclined to agree with our teetotal friends that the liberal supply of "Stroud water" laid on in some places in the town has more to do with it.

It rants on, '"Fetch forth the stocks! As I have life and honour, There shall he sit till noon" (Shakespeare) is now no empty threat, and we hope the folk of Painswick will for the future be content with being happy and glorious without getting uprorious [*sic*].'

Tetbury's curiously named Gumstool Hill is a tag that has stuck since the days it apparently housed the town's gumstool (or ducking stool) – a dreadful medieval contraption used for dunking unscrupulous traders and gobby females in the local pond or river. There's also a Duck Street at Winchcombe.

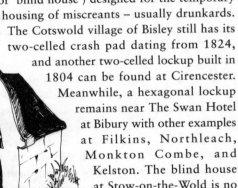

Overdo it in the local hostelry and you might find yourself sobering up in the local lockup – a windowless stone structure (also known as a 'round house' or 'blind house') designed for the temporary housing of miscreants – usually drunkards. The Cotswold village of Bisley still has its two-celled crash pad dating from 1824, and another two-celled lockup built in 1804 can be found at Cirencester. Meanwhile, a hexagonal lockup remains near The Swan Hotel at Bibury with other examples at Filkins, Northleach, Monkton Combe, and Kelston. The blind house at Stow-on-the-Wold is no longer around although, according to the Revd Mr D. Royce (writing in the mid-1800s), that particular home-from-home doesn't sound too bad; apparently, beer used to be fed through the grille to the rascals inside via a tobacco pipe.

HOME GAOL

An inquisitive delve into the county archives and newspapers soon reveals a diverting plethora of petty Cotswold crimes, some of them very petty indeed.

John Craddock Betteridge, a 'victualler' of Northleach, was fined £5 and 10s costs in August 1829 for 'allowing Bagatelle to be played in his house'; Charles Roberts, a boatman from Chalford, was fined 1s (and costs) for 'indecently easing his person' in King Street, Stroud in February 1851, and John Matthews and James Powell, two labourers from Stroud, got six months' hard labour for stealing 'about fifty cabbages' from a garden in Painswick on 19 May 1832.

June 1832 seems to have been a particularly bad month in Bisley. Elisabeth, wife of William Peyton, labourer, was fined 13s damages plus costs or two months in Horsley House of Correction for breaking twenty-six panes of glass in the house of widow Elizabeth Alder. Labourer Robert Lugg was fined 10s plus costs or two months' hard labour for trespassing on Bisley Common (while there, he nicked approximately 10 square yards of turf and soil belonging to the Lord of the Manor).

The legal procession preceding this particular Lent assize session, described in the *Stroud Free Press* in the mid-1800s, was obviously quite a show:

> About two hundred of the magistracy, gentry, and yeomanry of the county met High Sheriff, William Dent Esquire at Sudely [*sic*] Castle, where they partook of a substantial breakfast, and then escorted the High Sheriff in procession to Cheltenham en route for Gloucester. Preceded by the javelin men in their gay liveries of blue and silver, and under the sheriff's carriage, came the elegant carriage of the High Sheriff drawn by four splendid grey horses, and occupied by the sheriff and his chaplain, followed by the family carriage,

four in hand, about 200 horsemen, two abreast, and ten carriages containing private friends. This imposing *cortege* attracted wonder and admiration until it reached Cheltenham, where the townspeople and visitors were gathered in thousands to give it welcome.

Many naughty Cotsallers did their time at the Horsley House of Correction (built in the late 1700s on the site of an ancient priory). The prison was demolished in the nineteenth century although several properties in the Nailsworth area are said to have stones from the prison in their foundations.

Other offenders ended up at Northleach House of Correction – another one of four such buildings built in Gloucestershire at the time thanks to the reformist efforts of Sir George Onesiphorus Paul, Baronet. Sir George's memorial at Gloucester Cathedral declares, '…this county has become the example and model of the best system of criminal discipline in which provident regulation has banished the use of fetters and health been substituted for contagion thus happily reconciling humanity with punishment and the prevention of crime with individual reform.' Sir George is buried at Woodchester where a road, Paul's Rise, named after the great man, can also be found, along with a plaque. What remains of the old prison now serves as offices for the Cotswolds Conservation Board. A new 'Escape to the Cotswolds' discovery centre was opened in 2010 and there's also a bistro/café on site – occasionally patronised, so I'm told, by a mysterious figure dressed in black prison uniform and a top hat. (Check CCB website for opening times).

FOUR GRISLY COTSWOLD MURDERS

On 22 March 1743, Blacksmith Joseph Mutloe from Herefordshire was executed and hung in chains on Rodborough Hill for strangling widow Jane Clarke with a handkerchief and fracturing her skull with a Wool Card (a tool normally used to prepare fibre for spinning), before robbing her. As it happens, the famous Revd Mr George Whitefield was preaching in the vicinity at the time of the hanging – an event he describes in a letter dated 24 March 1743 as a 'miserable spectacle' attended by 'very violent' weather.

Edwin Jefferey, a butcher's assistant of Stow-on-the-Wold, bashed Mr Rens, French teacher and accountant to Stow Provident Bank, with a slaughterhouse stick before pinching his gold watch, which he then buried in a garden. He later made the mistake of taking the timepiece for repair, an action that eventually called time on his own short life. Jeffery was hanged for murder on 15 April 1835 aged just twenty-one.

Fast-forward half a century and it's the turn of another youngster, Edward Pritchard (aged twenty) from Stroud – hanged for the murder of fourteen-year-old Henry James Allen on his way to the Capital & Counties Bank on behalf of his employer. The hangman was James Berry of Bradford – infamous for the 'Babbacombe murder' horror at Exeter gaol, when the gallows equipment failed on no less than three occasions. No such luck for Pritchard. In a letter dated January 1887, Mr Berry states his terms of £10 (plus travelling expenses) for the execution – £5 if the condemned man is reprieved. There was no reprieve. A new rope was sent from Holloway by parcel post and a deeply penitent Pritchard swung on 17 February 1887.

Another Stroudie, Frederick Wyndham (aged forty-five) was executed just before Christmas 1893 for shooting his elderly father in the neck and chest at Oakridge. It seems Fred didn't approve of the old man's choice of girlfriend (Virtue Mills, aged forty-one) and would, by all accounts, liked to have had a pop at her too. The *Gloucester Journal* recorded Fred's final words: 'I wish you all goodbye. I should like to have killed that whore before I died.'

FIVE FEMALE FELONS

Anne Williams was burnt at the stake at Gloucester in April 1753 – the form of execution commonly employed for women who had killed their husbands or been found guilty of 'coining' (counterfeiting coins). Despite protesting her innocence ('with a Behaviour quite unbecoming her melancholy Departure' and 'her belly'), she was declared guilty of poisoning her unfortunate spouse with 'White Mercury', which she had mixed up in some 'Pap', causing the poor man to experience so much 'Vomitings and Purgings' that he pegged out the very next day (*Gloucester Journal*). Coincidentally, there's not much call for pap in the Cotswolds these days, although should you particularly wish to try it, I believe you should put wheat flour and buttermilk on your shopping list. Reference to this uninviting sounding dish is also made in an unflattering old local rhyme which runs along the lines, 'The Dursley baboon/As yet his pap without a spoon.'

By the time twenty-one-year-old Harriet Tarver of Chipping Campden was dispatched in April 1836 for murdering her husband, Thomas, the punishment of the day had been reduced to the supposedly more humane sentence of hanging. Mrs Tarver clearly also believed the way to stop a man's heart was through his stomach, for she laced her husband's rice pudding with arsenic having apparently been giddified by some other fellow's irresistible charms.

The demise of so-called witch Joan Perry 175 years earlier remains one of the Cotswolds' strangest and oft told tales – 'The Campden Wonder'. The elusive supposed victim of the story, William Harrison, steward to the Viscountess Campden, turned up alive about two years after Joan was hanged on Broadway Hill (along with her two sons) for his murder.

Ann Tye (aged thirty-eight) from Dowdeswell met her end on 4 May 1818 for murdering her 'bastard child'. At the time of her execution she is reported to have been so weak she had to be supported by one or two persons before being 'launched into eternity in view of an immense crowd of spectators' (*Gloucester Journal*).

Despite calls from the prosecution and the jury, thirty-three-year-old Charlotte Long from North Nibley was hanged in August 1833 for 'wilfully setting fire to three ricks of hay' using gunpowder. The account of her trial makes sorry reading, especially the report that, 'when first placed at the bar', the prisoner had 'an infant only a few weeks old, at the breast'. Just hours before facing the 'great crowds' (which included many women) gathered to witness the execution, Charlotte learned her baby was dead. Notwithstanding the gravity of the situation, the paper reports that pickpockets were at work 'under the very drop' and that a 'gentleman was robbed of his gold chain and seals' (*Gloucester Journal*).

THIRTEEN COTSWOLDIANS STRUNG UP FOR CRIMES OTHER THAN MURDER

Given that it was a hanging offence, a large number of offenders seem to have been brazen or desperate enough to consider stealing animals a risk worth taking. Among those Cotswold folk hanged for sheep stealing between 1795 and 1818 were:

William Large of Little Barrington – aged sixty
James Cornick of North Nibley – aged thirty-four
James Parsons of Bisley – aged twenty-seven
Henry Newport of Southrop – aged thirty-seven
Thomas Bishop of Fulbrook – aged twenty-nine
William Mason of Fulbrook – aged forty
James Gardiner of Eastleach Turville – aged thirty-three

Despite reportedly being 'so ill, weak and deeply affected' that they could 'scarcely live' to execution day, Stephen Cratchley, Joseph Wildey and Anselm Prinn were all hanged in January 1767 for their part in the famous bread riots at The Shambles in Stroud (Cratchley had carried a horn which he 'blew to collect the mob'). Wildey is reported to have been 'insensible' with a 'high fever', having suffered delirium for several days (*Gloucester Journal*).

George Dalby from Stroud (aged twenty) hanged in August 1789 for the rape of Elizabeth Paul. At his death he warned the crowd against the dangers of breaking the Sabbath – the source, apparently, of all his woes.

William Townley, a bad lot from Winchcombe (aged twenty-nine), faced the hangman on 23 March 1811 for burglary. The *Gloucester*

Journal reports that 'his behaviour prior and subsequent to his condemnation, exhibited an extraordinary degree of insensitivity and hardihood' and that 'his mind seemed entirely occupied by schemes for escaping from prison' – insisting right up to the moment of sacrament that he was not guilty of the crime. Unfortunately, his reprieve arrived just too late having been sent to the wrong place.

Joseph Stephens (aged thirty-three) of Minchinhampton seems to have been dealt a particularly harsh sentence. He was hanged in August 1800 for 'cutting cloth from the Tenters' of Messr Wathens of Woodchester.

YOUR MONEY OR YOUR LIFE! FOUR COTSWOLD HIGHWAYMEN

The *Gloucester Journal* of 1763 follows the story of a luckless, reckless highwayman called Daniel Neale, who made the fatal error of stopping off to have his horse shod at a blacksmith's in Chalfordbottom. Unfortunately for him, he was recognised and subsequently secured at The George in Bisley, where some chap who just happened to have been robbed that very morning ruined the highwayman's supper by obligingly popping in to provide a positive ID.

'And will you swear that?' demanded our villain. 'Why then, I may as well die first as last,' at which point he proceeded to cut his own throat 'in a shocking manner'. As if his day hadn't been bad enough, Neale didn't quite finish the job and although the paper grimly predicts that he 'could not live 'till night', this notorious fellow finally faced the gallows a few weeks later. Apparently, Neale 'expressed terrors at the approach of death, and seemed to think his sins had been too great to be expiated by so short a repentance, and prolonged the moment in which he was to be turned off to the very last.'

A rather well turned-out road agent springs to life in the pages of a 1774 edition of the *Gloucester Journal*. Despite being relieved of a guinea and a shilling in the parish of Edgeworth, his victim was obviously astute enough to notice he was wearing a 'light fustian frock, green waistcoat and breeches, a light two-curled wig, and a fan-tailed hat'. The account is rather less complimentary regarding the highwayman's face, describing him as 'marked with the small-pox' with 'a scar upon his chin'.

It appears the infamous highwayman William Crew of Wotton-Underedge [*sic*] had a serious dairy habit for he is reported as having pilfered his own grampy's cheesy wares on no less than three occasions in two weeks. Eventually, the old man put up security bars – a complete waste of time, for William simply used a rake to drag the cheese close enough to cut into smaller pieces. Sadly, this was by no means the sum of Crew's crimes, which were many and horrid. A 'wanted' notice appearing in the *Gloucester Journal* of 1786 offers a reward of ten guineas for his apprehension, describing him as a stout thirty-seven-year-old, 'of a pale complexion, dark brown hair, about five feet ten inches high', wearing 'in common a pompadour or sheep-russet coat'. Crew was eventually caught and hanged (along with his two colleagues) on 21 April 1786, for robbing the house of octogenarian Mrs Fowles of Huntley – badly beating her with a large stick. A reported 10,000 spectators turned up to hear the highwayman's exhortation to 'shun from sin' and see him swing – a moment dramatically punctuated by a 'two strong flashes of lightning...attended with thunder'.

As for the legendary highwayman Tom Long, apart from having a junction named after him on Minchinhampton Common (not to mention a Cotswold ale), this mysterious figure didn't leave many clues as to his actual existence. Still, never mind, there's plenty of folklore about Long in these parts, including tales of forbidden love and robbery on the Cotswold highways, culminating at a windswept Cotswold crossroads.

BROTHERHOOD OF CRIME

The brothers Willis were hanged on 22 August 1735 – Nathaniel for pinching a hanky and £25 in 'Silver and Gold', and the fashion-conscious Jonathan for stealing a pair of buckskin breeches and a dimity or fustian white waistcoat which, rather recklessly, was 'found upon him' (*Gloucester Journal*).

Two years later, in 1737, brothers John and Abraham Wood were condemned for highway robbery on the oath of Henry Lovell, 'on Suspicion' of relieving him of his silver and brass in the parish of Butherop.

They say bad things come in threes – definitely true in the case of the infamous Dunsdon brothers – Tom, Dick and Harry – who plagued the poor folk around the Wychwood Forest area of the Cotswolds in the late 1700s. Henry and Thomas were eventually hanged in July 1784 for 'Felonously Assaulting William Harding on 31 May' at the parish of Widford. Following execution at Over, near Gloucester, their bodies were gibbeted near to the scene of the crime. The story goes that Dick had earlier been rendered armless, thanks to a bungled robbery attempt at a manor house near Burford. Having reached through an opening of a door, he found himself shaking hands with an awaiting welcoming party. No doubt his captors were mightily pleased with themselves to have trapped such a rogue – although they only had the slippery character for as long as it took Tom and Harry to chop off his arm.

Avening brothers Matthew and Henry Pinnell were executed in April 1829 for the violent robbery of farmer James Kearsey, on his way back from Tetbury market. One of them beat the poor man in 'a most dreadful manner' until he fell off his horse whereupon they declared 'stop and deliver', before running away with 'four £5 notes, forty £1 notes, several memorandums, some silver, a key and his watch'. An account of the trial and execution published at the time reports that the brothers were attended at their execution by the Revd Mr Ordinary, whose 'endeavours to prepare them for a future existence' had been 'unceasing'. So much for latrociny.

TWO GOT AWAY, FIVE SENT AWAY

Okay, so he might not have been in the same league as Captain Jack Sparrow, but according to the history books, Henry Brydges, wild child of 'John Lord Chaundos Baron of Sheudley' apparently took the rap for his share of 'arming and supplying' the *Salamander* of Bristol and the *Mary Grace* of Penzance with 'food, gunpowder, pikes, darts and other weapons of warlike nature' against the *Whalefish* of Denmark, for which misdemeanours he was pardoned by James I in 1611. He's also said to have had a pretty eventful sideline as a highwayman. Despite all this excitement, Henry eventually settled for a quiet life in the sleepy Cotswold village of Avening. His elegant memorial hangs in the Bridges' aisle at the Church of the Holy Cross, where he looks suitably contrite.

Hidden in a quiet section of St Laurence's in Stroud is the grave of twenty-one-year-old Joseph Francis Delmont, Lieutenant of His Majesty's 82nd Regiment, who met his end following a duel on 18 August 1807 precipitated by a petty row with a fellow recruiting officer. According to the story told by Stroud historian Paul Hawkins

Fisher (died in 1873) in his *Notes and Recollections of Stroud*, Lieutenant Benjamin Heazle apparently opened fire before Delmont turned round, mortally wounding his colleague, before slinking off – perhaps overseas. Delmont died a few days later, Fisher recording the dreadful possibility that his death may have been hastened as a result of the actions of a nurse who mistakenly fed the desperate man a lotion meant for his wounds.

Foreign climes were also the destination of Cotswold watchmaker Giles Coates, who was caught 'in the unlawful pursuit of Game' at Weekly Wood in the parish of Chedworth in 1833, whereupon he shot at Lord Stowell's gamekeeper, setting his jacket alight and wounding his left side. Despite legging it to London, Coates was eventually apprehended and sentenced to death by hanging, although he ended up being deported instead. Unfortunately, the convict ship he sailed on (*George III*) was shipwrecked off the coast of Tasmania and the watchmaker was believed to have drowned, although intriguing leads pursued by some of his descendants in recent years perhaps hint otherwise. Whether Giles made it or not, it appears Van Diemen's Land wasn't short of a few Chedworthians. Among those also deported there around that time were Joshua Stevens in 1831, Jacob Mustoe in 1832 and James Joy in 1835. A clock thought to have been made either by Giles or his father, featuring an unusual printed dial on white enamel with a date window and the words 'Coates, Chedworth', can be seen at Gloucester City Museum and Art Gallery.

The bell-ringers of St James the Great in Dursley are among those that still ring the traditional Pancake Bell on Shrove Tuesday, although they're unable to confirm whether one William Champion, a former Dursley hatter, ever took part in this charming tradition. One thing's for sure, Mr Champion certainly knew how to handle a bell. Having been deported to Hobart Town in 1823 for receiving stolen goods, subsequent newspaper reports describe him as a master bell-ringer, whose cash and expertise enabled the 'first peal of bells in the southern hemisphere' at Holy Trinity Church in 1847. He's also noted as being the first Tasmanian beaver (making hats from the hair and wool of silver-haired rabbits) and for owning 'The Jolly Hatter'.

6

CULTURAL COTSWOLDS: MUSIC, FILM & STAGE

CLASSICS, CAROLS & HYMNS

Composer Dr Ralph Vaughan Williams OM was born at the Old Vicarage in the Cotswold village of Down Ampney (after which he named one of his hymn tunes) near Cirencester in 1872. Vaughan Williams senior was minister there from 1868 until his death in 1875. A beautiful stained-glass window featuring the resurrection is dedicated to his memory and an excellent exhibition on the life of the composer can be found at the back of the church.

Composer (Brian) Cornelius Cardew (died in 1981) was born near Winchcombe.

Composer Gerald Finzi (born in 1901) lived at Painswick from July 1922 to February 1926. 'A Severn Rhapsody' and 'Requiem da Camera' are just two of the works he composed during this Cotswold period.

Composer Charles Wilfred Orr (born in Cheltenham 1893) also made the 'Queen of the Cotswolds' his home, living there from 1934 until his death in 1976. Perhaps best known for his delightful song settings (many to the poetry of A.E. Housman), he also wrote a composition for string orchestra entitled 'A Cotswold Hill-Tune'. A blue plaque at Painswick marks the composer's final home.

Award-winning classical, film and television composer Geoffrey Burgon (died in 2010) lived at Lypiatt near Bisley for many years – his huge musical legacy includes numerous classical works as well as well-known themes for such film and TV productions as *Tinker, Tailor, Soldier, Spy*, *Monty Python's Life of Brian* and *Brideshead Revisited*. His critically acclaimed 'Requiem' was premiered at the Three Choirs Festival in 1976.

Composer Peter Maxwell Davies (later Sir Peter) ran the music department at Cirencester Grammar School between 1959 and 1962. During this time he composed and arranged many pieces for children's choirs and school orchestras, including a setting of 'O Magnum Mysterium' which was premiered in December 1960 at St John Baptist, Cirencester, by the chorus and orchestra of Cirencester Grammar School with the late (Edward) Allan Wicks CBE at the organ.

Gustav Holst's setting of Christina Rossetti's 'In the Bleak Midwinter' is dedicated to Cranham, also to his mother, Clara née Lediard, who died when Gustav was seven. Clara (originally from Cirencester) once lived in Cranham and played the harmonium in the church. Tradition has it that the composer wrote the carol while snowbound during a visit to the village. The piece certainly came into its own during the dreadful weather conditions of 1961/2 when the lines, 'Snow had fallen, snow on snow, snow on snow', are reported to have been sung at the local church 'with particular verve' (*Stroud News*). Holst (born in Cheltenham) also wrote the haunting melody to medieval carol 'Lullay My Liking' and his 'Cotswold Symphony' was written in 1900.

According to the evergreen *Oxford Book of Carols* (first published 1928), the 'Gloucestershire Wassail' (pronounced locally as 'waysail') was sung to the book's co-producer, Ralph Vaughan Williams, 'by an old person in the county'. Unlike the orchard wassail carried out in other parts of the country, the 'Gloucestershire Wassail' was a house-to-house Christmas custom, rather like carol singing. Variations of the piece were collected at two Cotswold villages by folklore revivalist/collector Cecil Sharp, and a version of 'The Holly and the Ivy' was gathered at Chipping Campden.

Another Campden related carol may well have been lost forever were it not for the tenacity of local singer-songwriter Johnny Coppin, who discovered an extract of the four-verse 'Campden Carol' at the Gloucester archives in the late 1980s. The piece was duly completed, arranged and recorded by Coppin and fellow musician Paul Burgess in 1990.

The Revd Mr John Keble was born at Fairford in 1792. Perhaps best known as the author of *The Christian Year* (first published in 1827) and a founder member of the so-called Oxford Movement, Keble was curate of the Cotswold churches of Eastleach Martin, Eastleach Turville and Southrop for periods during the 1800s as well as assistant curate at his father's church at St John the Baptist, Coln St Aldwyns, from 1825 to 1835. Many of his poetry verses appear as hymns in such publications as *The English Hymnal* and *Hymns Ancient & Modern*. Keble College, Oxford, was founded in his memory and two memorial windows to John Keble senior and junior can be found in the church at Coln St Aldwyns.

The Revd Mr Benjamin Beddome (born in 1717) was pastor of the Baptist church at Bourton-on-the-Water – a place he evidently loved. He was there for more than fifty years. Beddome's prolific hymn-writing output included a volume of over 800 compositions, many perhaps written as part of his custom of producing a hymn to follow his Sunday morning sermons.

Other hymn-writers with Cotswold links include Thomas Coles (born near Winchcombe), the Revd Mr Benjamin Francis (died in 1799) based over the hills at Shortwood, and William Freeman Lloyd (born in 1791) from Uley, who wrote the hymn 'My Times Are In Thy Hand'.

The following Cotswold villages all lend their names to hymn tunes penned by composer John Barnard: Yanworth, Chedworth, Widford and Guiting Power (usually sung to the hymn 'Christ Triumphant Ever Reigning'), Coln Rogers, Asthall, Little Barrington, Stanton, Stanton Harcourt, Temple Guiting, Fossebridge and Coln St Dennis. The Cotswold village of Oakridge Lynch is also immortalised in the name of a hymn tune by composer, Dr Martin Shaw OBE (died in 1958). Oakridge Lynch was also the country home of hymn writer, Percy Dearmer.

Hymn writer Mary Peters (*née* Bowly) was born in Cirencester in 1813. Among the many hymns she composed were 'Through the Love of God our Saviour' and 'Our God Is Light'.

ROCKING COTSWOLDS

Somewhat at the other end of the musical scale, legendary drummer Cozy Powell was also born in Cirencester. Among the myriad bands/musicians he worked with were Rainbow, Whitesnake and Black Sabbath. One of his solo singles, 'Dance with the Devil', made it to number three in the UK singles charts. Sadly, Powell's career was cut short by a fatal car accident near Bristol in 1998.

A little known group called The Beatles played Stroud Subscription Rooms in the early 1960s, supported by the Rebel Rousers. The council politely requested 'no Teddy Boys' and asked the 'Ladies' attending not to wear stiletto heels.

Not long afterwards, the people of Stroud were treated to a dramatic Sub Rooms appearance by Screaming Lord Sutch and the Savages, the self-styled 3rd Lord of Harrow making his entrance in a large black coffin.

The unassuming little Baptist church at Bourton played host to a whole cast of musical greats at a number of impromptu concerts organised and presented by Cotswold musician Gordon Jackson during the 1990s – an unexpected treat for the village's somewhat awestruck residents, as well as those local musos privileged enough to share the stage. Performers included Steve Winwood, the late Jim Capaldi, Ruby Turner, Mike Kellie, Michael J. McEvoy, Robbie Blunt, Tony Hinnigan, Bill Zorn, Roscoe 'G', Narada Michael Walden and Jess Roden.

Brazilian guitarist José Neto's album *Live at Guiting Power* (1998) was recorded live at, well, Guiting Power (in the village hall, actually).

Bass player John Entwistle of The Who died in Las Vegas in 2002. His funeral was held at Stow-on-the-Wold where the musician had lived for many years. A subsequent auction of property from the star's former mansion, held by Sotherby's, featured an eclectic array of items from a pink Fender Precision bass guitar to the cast of a Mako shark.

'Up-and-coming Irish band' U2 played the Marshall Rooms, Stroud, in 1980 although, unfortunately, the event was disrupted by the jeering and heckling of a 'moronic minority'. The band eventually walked off during 'Stories for Boys' and never came back (*Stroud News*).

FESTIVAL FEVER

Despite having several world-renowned music festivals on its doorstep (e.g. Cheltenham Music Festival, Three Choirs Festival and Bath Festivals), the Cotswolds boasts an impressive classical constellation of its own including (not exhaustive):

• Bledington Music Festival – founded 2001. President: Thomas Trotter, Vice President: Catrin Finch
• Chipping Campden Music Festival – founded 2002. President: Paul Lewis, Patron of Education Programme: Julian Lloyd Webber
• Chipping Norton Music Festival – celebrating its 100th festival in March 2012
• Cirencester Organ Festival (bi-annual from 2011) – founded 2010 after the re-building of the 'Father' Henry Willis organ at St John Baptist
• Cotswold Early Music Festival – founded 1999
• Guiting Festival – founded 1970. Honorary President: Joanna MacGregor.
• Naunton Music Society – founded approximately 1984. Patron: Dame Felicity Lott DBE
• Tetbury Music Festival – founded 2003. Patron: HRH The Prince of Wales. Artistic Adviser: Steven Isserlis CBE
• Windrush Chamber Music Festival (held in Burford) – founded 2009. Artistic director: Sholto Kynoch
• Wotton Concert Series – founded 2010. Musical advisers: Ben Hoffnung, Catherine Wyn-Rogers

WISH I'D BEEN THERE

Notwithstanding such a cornucopia of modern-day musical choice, there are some once-in-a-lifetime Cotswold performances one just can't help rue missing, including:

An extravaganza in May 1859 at the King's Head, Cirencester, billed as 'The greatest musical wonder of the age', featuring Organophanist Mr W.T. Park, 'ranging in his voice the extraordinary Compass of four octaves, imitating the Clarionet, Piccolo, and Bagpipes'. Also, tenor Mynheer Van Foot, who reportedly received 5,000 guilders from the King of Holland in recognition of his 'superiority as a Ballad Singer.' (*Wilts & Gloucestershire Standard*)

A performance 'to great acclaim' by violinist, 'Mr Willy' at Stroud's Subscription Rooms in November 1851. The newspaper review is positively glowing: 'His instrument is evidently the organ of his soul,' it says, although accompanist (Mr John Willy) does draw some criticism for 'slightly concealing Mr Willy's more refined passages', particularly on, 'Oh! no we never mention her.' (*Stroud Free Press*)

A visit to the local Salvation Army corps by world-wide travellers, vocalists and instrumentalists Major and Mrs Tom Plant in April 1910. Major Plant is credited with inventing many unique instruments including a 7ft-high instrument consisting of several hundred tubes made of a composition of bell-metal and aluminium, producing a 'liquid sound' which 'when manipulated to its fullest extent closely resembles a grand organ' (*Evesham Journal & Four Shires Advertiser*).

TREADING THE BOARDS

The Salvation Army also features in the story of a charming little theatre at Chipping Norton, which served as the town's citadel until the early 1960s. Its foundation stones, laid by Commander Herbert Booth and Major Oliphant in 1888, can still be seen. Following a spell as a furniture warehouse, the building's potential was eventually spotted in 1973 by Royal Shakespeare Company actors John and Tamara Malcolm, through whose efforts 'The Theatre' was officially opened by actor Tom Baker (then Dr Who) on 29 August 1975.

The Cotswolds has its own opera house – Longborough Festival Opera (Patron: Lady Valerie Solti). Converted from a former barn, the grand theatre has 500 seats (which once graced the Royal

Opera House, Covent Garden) and an orchestra pit large enough to accommodate up to sixty-five musicians.

The Cotswolds' professional touring theatre celebrated its twenty-fifth anniversary in 2010. The Festival Players Theatre Company (consisting of up to eight professional actors playing all the parts) performs open-air Shakespeare all over the country.

The Cotswold Players were formed in 1911 by author and founder of the International Lyceum Club, Constance Smedley (died in 1941). She and her husband, the artist Maxwell Armfield, once lived at Amberley, near Stroud.

The actor, singer and composer Edwin Ransford (died in 1876) was born at Bourton-on-the-Water. Having started out as an extra in the chorus at Haymarket, his later career included appearances at Covent Garden, Drury Lane and the English Opera House.

Another famous Bourton son, Wilfrid Hyde-White, was born at the rectory there in 1903. His illustrious TV and film career included the film *My Fair Lady* (starring such luminaries as Audrey Hepburn, Rex Harrison and Stanley Holloway) in which Hyde-White co-starred as the character Colonel Pickering.

Later described as 'the greatest tragic genius the stage has seen' (Hannam-Clark), struggling Victorian actor Edmund Kean tied the knot with actress Mary Chambers at Stroud parish church on 17 July 1808 – a marriage that, sadly, didn't last.

Actor James (Jimmy) Edwards DFC (well known for his Pa Glum character in the BBC radio comedy *Take It From Here*, not to mention many others) was stationed at Down Ampney during the Second World War. His heroic action at Arnhem in 1944 earned him the Distinguished Flying Cross.

Actor, comedian and writer Ronald (Ronnie) Barker OBE (died in 2005) opened and ran an antiques shop called The Emporium at Chipping Norton for several years during his retirement.

Actor Donald Ellis Pickering died at Eastleach in 2009 and film director Michael Powell (died in 1990) is buried at Avening. An inscription on his distinctive gravestone reads 'Film Director and Optimist'.

THE CHRISTMAS PLAY

Traditional mummers would have been a common sight at Christmas time:

> Here comes I, old Father Christmas, Christmas or not,
> I hope old Father Christmas will never be forgot.
> A room, make room here gallant boys, and give us room to rhyme,
> We've come to show activity upon a Christmas time.
> Acting youth or acting age, the like was never acted on this stage;
> If you don't believe what I now say, enter the King of France, and clear the way!'

(Excerpt from the old Winchcombe play)

Most villages had their own play or at least attracted a visit from a neighbouring village troupe acting out their ancient folk performance. Unfortunately, few plays survived the First World War and were sadly lost or forgotten, though, thanks to many dedicated researchers, just like their own resurrection themed plots, several Cotswold plays have been triumphantly and fittingly revived in recent years and are once again contributing to the spirit of Christmas. Marshfield (Gloucestershire), Bampton and Headington (Oxfordshire) still perform their old village plays. Chipping Campden has just revived its traditional play and successful revival plays are also performed in many more locations including Chedworth, Dursley, Bisley, Winchcombe, the Stroud Valleys, the Forest of Dean, Cheltenham, Tewkesbury, Gloucester and Oxford.

SNOW JOKE

Strange though it may seem, Ebley near Stroud experiences more snow than the rest of the Cotswolds put together. Actually – it's more snow-fake than snow flake but I bet you didn't notice when you last went to the movies. 'Snow Business' has been busy making wintery stuff for film, television, live events and visual merchandising for twenty-five years and is now a centre of excellence for snow effects throughout the world, boasting a blizzard of credits including such block-busters as *Harry Potter*, *Band of Brothers* and *Gladiator*.

STAR STRUCK COTSWOLDS

Given its shapely contours and ageless beauty, it's hardly surprising the camera loves the Cotswolds. Some of the many film/TV programmes featuring parts of the region include:

Bridget Jones's Diary (2001)
Cider with Rosie (TV)
Die Another Day (2002)
Doctor Doolittle (1967)
Dracula (TV)
Dulcima (1971)
Emma (TV)
Heavy Weather (TV)
Jeeves & Wooster (TV)
Joseph Andrews (1977)
Lark Rise to Candleford (TV)
Martin Chuzzlewit (TV)
Meet the Ancestors (TV)
Memphis Belle (1990)
Miss Marple (TV)
Our Mutual Friend (TV)
Rip Van Winkle (silent)
Stardust (2007)
Tawny Pipit (1944)
Tess of the d'Urbervilles (2008)

The Canterbury Tales (1972)
The Famous Five (TV)
The Libertine (2004)
The Mayor of Casterbridge (TV)
TV's *Most Haunted*
The Titfield Thunderbolt (1953)
The Wyvern Mystery (TV)
Vanity Fair (TV)

COTSCELEBS – HONORARY COTSWOLDIANS

I'm not sure what the latest benchmark is before a so-called 'incomer' can rightfully consider themselves a local (last time I heard, it was about forty years) but never mind all that. With the likes of Kate Moss, Elizabeth Hurley and Kate Winslet among the starry host of celebrities favouring the Cotswolds, the region clearly retains its long-established magnetism for 'creative types'! And of course, not only are the Cotswolds a top celebrity destination of choice, they also have impeccable royal credentials. The Prince of Wales and The Duchess of Cornwall, as well as The Princess Royal, have country residences in the Cotswolds.

7

ROYALS, WRITERS
& ALL THE REST

MORE RIGHT ROYAL COTSWOLD
CONNECTIONS

Tradition has it that the re-building of the exquisite church of the Holy Cross, Avening, was commissioned to salve the guilty conscience of a bitter little queen. A hawk-mews at Avening Court was once held by one Brittric (Lord of Gloucester) whose misfortune it was to be sent on a diplomatic mission to Flanders, where Count Baldwin's young daughter, Matilda, took a shine to him. Unfortunately, it seems Brittric gave her the old brush-off – a mistake which was to cost him dearly. Matilda finally settled for her distant cousin, the Duke of Normandy (later King William the Conqueror) whom she persuaded in true 'woman scorned' fashion to confiscate Brittric's estates and check him into prison, which is where the poor fellow sadly died. A subsequent guilt trip prompted Matilda to commission the re-building of Avening's church, the consecration of which was marked by a royal treat for the workers, consisting of boar's head – hence Avening's celebrated 'Pig Face Day', still observed in the village today. A wall-mounted plaque outside the Church of the Holy Cross records that trees were planted in December 1980 to commemorate the 900th anniversary of its consecration.

The final resting place of Henry VIII's last wife, Katherine Parr, is at Sudeley where she died in 1548, seven days after giving birth to her only child, the Lady Mary. Unfortunately, the Dowager Queen's remains suffered many less-than-royal indignities over the years, before finally being removed to a stone vault in 1817 away from 'the eye of the inquisitive and the vulgar' (Dent).

Queen Elizabeth I was actually a balding, red-haired bachelor from Bisley – or so some would still have you believe. The tradition goes

that the young princess died while staying at Over Court in the village, prompting her protectors to substitute a local child in her place. Unfortunately, they could only find a boy – which conveniently explains why Queen Bess never married. Whoever he or she was, Queen Elizabeth was no stranger to the Cotswolds. While visiting Sudeley Castle on one of her famous 'progresses', she was presented with a bit of wool (Cotswold, of course) by an old shepherd – something, no doubt, she had always wanted.

Edward 'The Black Prince' was born at Woodstock in 1330; Charles Beauclerk (illegitimate son of King Charles II by Nell Gwynn) was created first Earl of Burford; King Athelstan (died in 939) is buried at Malmesbury Abbey; the Dowager Queen Mary was 'evacuated' to Badminton during the Second World War and more than one Cotswold inn claims to have provided B&B hospitality to King Charles I.

WORDS & PICTURES BY

The Cotswolds' irreplaceable Laurie Lee MBE (died in 1997) is sadly missed although, his memory burns particularly brightly in the Stroud Valleys where, among many local remembrances, a hoppy Cotswold bitter bears his name, and his likeness appears on the £10 note of the Stroud Pound – a local currency launched in September 2009. The famous *Cider with Rosie* author is buried at Slad. One side of his headstone simply states, 'He lies in the valley he loved', while the poem 'April Rise' is engraved on the other, a green and lemon blossoming bush perfectly illustrating this much-loved poet's timelessly evocative words.

Not far away at Miserden rests Laurie Lee's long time friend, the author and 'Cotswold Poet' Frank Mansell (died in 1979), remembered for his beautiful 'Cotswold Ballads', first published 1969, not to mention his 'deadly' fast bowling for the Sheepscombe Cricket Club, whose quirky cricket pitch, set on the brow of a hill above a steep hillside, has attracted much attention over the years. A downward slope begins just below the square with the outfield falling away so steeply that the poor old leg fielder often has no idea what's going on above and has to rely on his team-mates to herald the ball's imminent arrival. The site, known as the 'Laurie Lee Field', was purchased by Lee in 1971.

Author Mary Roberts aka 'The Beautiful Duchess' grew up in Painswick. Her book *Annals of my Village: being a Calendar of Nature, for Every Month in the Year*, published in 1831, was based on the nearby village of Sheepscombe. Listed among her other works are the *Select Female Biography; comprising memoirs of eminent British ladies, derived from original and other authentic sources*, *The Wonders of the Vegetable Kingdom displayed in a Series of Letters* and *A Popular History of the Mollusca*.

Novelist C.J. Cutcliffe Hyne (died in 1944), well-known for such works as *The Lost Continent: The Story of Atlantis* and his famous 'Captain Kettle' stories was born at Arlington, near Bibury.

Popular children's writer (Amy) Violet Needham, whose first published work was *The Black Riders* (1939), lived for approximately fifteen years at Horton near Little Sodbury where she died on 8 June 1967. Her name, followed by the title 'Authoress', appears on a tombstone at St James the Elder, Horton, along with that of her sister who died the very next day. The Violet Needham Society was founded in 1985 and has produced a limited edition of Miss Needham's last completed novel, *The Sword of St Cyprian*.

A framed notice on the organ of St Michael's in Duntisbourne Rouse records that the instrument was given in memory of the writer Katherine Mansfield (died in 1923) by her three sisters, one of whom lived in the village for many years. Two of the sisters are buried there.

Theological writer the Revd Mr Charles Buck was born at Hillesley in 1771. His collection *Anecdotes, Religious, Moral, and Entertaining:*

Alphabetically Arranged, and Interspersed with a Variety of Useful Observations ran to several editions. On the subject of 'Learned Females' he observes, 'Ladies have sometimes distinguished themselves as prodigies of learning', arguing that there are 'radical powers in the female sex as well as the male'.

The 'Super-tramp' poet and writer W.H. Davies (who famously lost a leg as a result of train-jumping in Canada) spent the last few years of his life at Nailsworth, finally settling at Glendower, where a plaque quotes from his popular poem 'Leisure': 'What is this life if, full of care.' Another plaque (featuring his poem 'Nailsworth') can be seen in the town's library.

Poet Sydney Dobell ended his days in 1874 at Horsley, near Nailsworth and is buried at Painswick, while J. Meade Falkner (died in 1932), author of the popular book *Moonfleet*, among others, rests at Burford.

The Cotswold village of Sezincote is mentioned in Sir John Betjeman's 'Summoned by Bells', and Adlestrop is immortalised in verse by Edward Thomas.

Novelist P.C. Wren (died in 1941), best known for his novel *Beau Geste*, is buried at Amberley near Stroud, which also features as 'Enderley' in the Victorian novel *John Halifax, Gentleman*, written by the best-selling Victorian writer, Dinah Mulock (Mrs Craick).

The remains of four of the six famous Mitford sisters rest at Swinbrook (along with 'Farve' and 'Muv'). Nancy's gravestone describes her as 'Authoress' and features a charming engraving of a mole.

The Revd Mr Wilbert Vere Awdry OBE, famous for his children's railway stories, retired to the Cotswolds. He died at Rodborough in 1997. A colourful window at St Mary Magdalene in Rodborough (in memory of the Revd Mr Awdry and his wife, Margaret) features a cameo of Thomas the Tank Engine in the bottom right-hand corner.

Best-selling author Joanna Trollope OBE was born in the Cotswolds, while celebrated poet and writer U.A. Fanthorpe CBE FRSL lived and died at Wotton-under-Edge. The writer Evelyn Waugh (died in 1966) lived at Stinchcombe near Dursley for nearly two decades and former Poet Laureate John Masefield (died in 1967) lived near Sapperton for a period in the 1930s.

Poet John Oldham (died in 1683) was born at Shipton Moyne and spent part of his education at Tetbury's grammar school. 'Pope's Seat' at Cirencester Park is named after the poet Alexander Pope, who assisted the first Earl Bathurst with the park's development, and Geoffrey Chaucer's son is said to have lived at Woodstock, not forgetting the legend that the great bard himself may have had links with the Dursley area.

The painter Sir William Llewellyn PRA was born at Cirencester in 1858. Sir William was president of the Royal Academy of Arts from December 1928 to December 1938.

Stained glass artist Mary Lowndes was born at the Rectory of Poole Keynes in the mid-1800s (Richard Lowndes was vicar there from 1854 to 1862). Unfortunately, there aren't any of her windows at the quaint little church of St Michael & All Angels, although perhaps she once admired some of its lovely stained glass.

Colleagues in life and companions in death – underneath the ancient yew trees at Sapperton lies a group of friends who once crafted exquisite things, influenced and inspired by the charismatic Cotswold beauty they found all around them. Now these famous fellow workers rest side-by-side in St Kenelm's tranquil graveyard, little altered since the days when Ernest Gimson and the Barnsley brothers, Sidney and Ernest, were ardent disciples of the Arts and Crafts movement of the late nineteenth and early twentieth century – heavily influenced by its famous proponent, William Morris. Gimson's chief cabinetmaker/foreman, Peter van der Waals (died in 1937), is buried in the graveyard at Christ Church, Chalford. Arts and Crafts etcher, illustrator, draughtsman and stalwart friend of the Cotswolds, Frederick Griggs, lived and died (1938) at Chipping Campden and William Morris (died in 1896) is buried at Kelmscott. An important collection of Arts and Crafts work is displayed at Cheltenham Art Gallery and Museum.

Celebrated sculptor Lynn Chadwick CBE lived in the Cotswolds for many years until his death at Lypiatt Park in 2003.

John Singer Sargent's famous oil painting 'Carnation, Lily, Lily Rose', set in a Broadway garden, can be seen at Tate Britain, London. William G. Simmonds (died in 1968) settled at Far Oakridge in the 1920s and Sir William Rothenstein (died in 1945) also lived there.

'Pre-Raphaelite' painter Frank Cadogan Cowper RA worked in the Cotswolds in later life. His famous 'Ugly Duckling' painting, featuring a pretty young woman dressed in a pink gown, was bequeathed to 'Cheltenham and its people' by the well-known antique dealer Ronald Summerfield and is now displayed at the Cheltenham Art Gallery and Museum (along with an interesting film about its sitter). In 1950 Valerie Tarantolo (then Anderson) was working as a shop assistant in Cirencester when spotted by the artist who asked her to sit for him. Over half a century later Valerie (now living in America) returned to England to see her portrait, having discovered its whereabouts after many years of searching.

YET MORE NOTABLE FOLK WITH COTSWOLD CONNECTIONS

The Victorian botanical artist and traveller Marianne North (born in 1830 in Hastings) ended her days at Alderley, near Wotton-under-Edge. The Marianne North Gallery at Kew Gardens, London, has recently undergone a major restoration and all 833 of her paintings (featuring more than 900 plant species) housed there have been conserved and restored.

'Father of English Geology' William 'Strata' Smith (born in 1769 at Churchill, Oxfordshire) lived in The Square at Stow-on-the-Wold for four years during the late 1700s. His pioneering geological map of Britain was published in 1815. A commemorative plaque recording his link with the town can be found at Stow and there are further memorials at Churchill and Midford.

A charming public garden in the centre of Chipping Campden commemorates the life of celebrated plant collector and writer Ernest Henry 'Chinese' Wilson, born in the town in 1876. Among his many hundreds of botanical introductions to the west was the 'Chinese gooseberry', commonly known as the kiwi fruit.

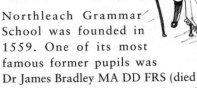

Northleach Grammar School was founded in 1559. One of its most famous former pupils was Dr James Bradley MA DD FRS (died in 1762) who succeeded Edmund Halley as Astronomer Royal in 1742. Dr Bradley was born at Sherborne, where a plaque at St Mary Magdalene commemorates his discoveries of the 'Aberration of Light and Nutation'. Another plaque can be found at Holy Trinity, Minchinhampton, his place of burial.

Civil engineer Sir Benjamin Baker KCB KCMC FRS (died in 1907), famous for his work on London's first underground railways, the Aswan Dam and Forth Bridge, rests at St Nicholas', Idbury, in the Oxfordshire Cotswolds, underneath an elaborate tomb complete with four flying buttresses.

Edward Wathen Fyffe of banana fame was born at Woodchester in 1853 and grew up in the nearby village of Box and Thomas Twining, founder of the famous Twinings tea company, was born at Painswick in 1675.

Renowned philosopher and physicist John Canton MA FRS was born in Stroud in 1718. A memorial plaque at The Shambles in Stroud records his attendance at a former school there.

A blue plaque at Chipping Norton commemorates the Revd Mr Edward Stone (born in 1702) who discovered salicylic acid, the active ingredient in aspirin, while living there.

Astronomer and mathematician, Charles Mason of the USA's Mason-Dixon Line fame was born near Stroud.

The Wellcome Trust Sanger Institute is named after Double Nobel Laureate Dr Frederick Sanger FRS OM CH, who was born at Rendcomb, near Cirencester, in 1918.

The champion flat-race jockey Fred Archer was born at Prestbury in 1857. The English international cricketer (retired) and artist Robert Charles 'Jack' Russell MBE FRSA was born in Stroud. The former England batsman Walter (Wally) Hammond (died in 1965) attended Cirencester Grammar School.

While on the subject of ball games, the cloth for many of the world's snooker tables and tennis balls is made in Stroud, and the rules for the game of croquet were codified at Chastleton near Moreton-in-Marsh by Walter Whitmore-Jones, who compiled a set of rules known as the 'Field Rules', published in *The Field* in 1866.

GREAT NAMES

Valentine Strong (died in 1662) was a notable Cotswold stonemason who built (among other things) the beautiful manor house at Lower Slaughter (now a hotel). He also worked on Sherborne House, near Northleach, once owned by another 'Great Name' – Sir John 'Crump' Dutton, so-called because of his hunched back.

Scrope Berdmore Davies (born in 1782) was a dandy and friend of Lord Byron whose colourful, all-embracing lifestyle cannot have brought much pleasure to his father, the rector of Horsley and later Tetbury.

Colonel Sir Percival Scrope Marling, 3rd Baronet VC CB was born at King's Stanley in 1861. The following five Victoria Cross holders were also born in the Cotswolds in the nineteenth-century: Eugene Paul

Bennett (Stroud), John Bythesea (Freshford), William Edgar Holmes (Wood Stanway), Alfred Ernest Ind (Tetbury) and Dudley Graham Johnson (Bourton-on-the-Water).

Adolphus Trotman was a hairpin manufacturer from Painswick who went out with a bang in 1873 as a result of experimenting with gases.

Sir Bevil Grenville was a Royalist commander who was mortally wounded at the Battle of Lansdown on 5 July 1643. A monument commemorating his heroism can be found at Lansdown Hill near Bath.

Pharaoh Webb was once the owner of Nailsworth's Egypt Mill (now a hotel & restaurant), which is one theory for how it got the name. Another suggests that it's a reference to the Red Sea from the time when the stream-straddling mill was used to dye cloth, thus colouring the water.

Ferdinando Tracey Travel was once rector of the parish of Upper Slaughter. He was followed by three members of the Witts family who, between them, served for 106 years (although none of them served as long as John Elliot – vicar of Randwick for seventy-two years from 1819). Thomas Trewpenny, Trethewy Tooker, Henry Bonny, Nicholas Botercram, Morice Holyday, William Woky and John Gellibrond are just a few more divine names you may come across on a Cotswolds tour.

Troylus Kingscote was a 'Comander [*sic*] for the Prince of Orange 40 yeares [*sic*]'. His grave at St John the Baptist in Kingscote states that he died in 1656 at the age of eighty. Incidentally, the first skirmish of the 'Glorious Revolution' took place at Cirencester following the landing of the Prince of Orange in 1688.

'Honest Jhon Stockwell' was buried on 25 September 1665 at Withington, having 'dyed of the plagve [*sic*]' the previous day. His headstone was rescued from the churchyard in 1985 and can now be seen inside the Easter Sepulchre of St Michael & All Angels.

Grey Brydges was the 5th Baron Chandos (died in 1621). He lived at Sudeley Castle in such grand style that it earned him an extra title – 'King of the Cotswolds'.

SIX INVENTORS WITH COTSWOLD CONNECTIONS

In 1815 John Lewis of Brimscombe patented the rotary shearing machine used to crop the surface of cloth in the local textile mills, which, in turn, inspired Edward Beard Budding to invent the first mechanical lawnmower at Stroud in 1830. Examples of both can be seen at Stroud's Museum in the Park, as well the modern screw thread adjustable spanner – also invented by Edward Budding.

Sir Issac Pitman (born in 1813) once lived at Orchard Street, Wotton-under-Edge, where a plaque commemorates the invention of his system of shorthand known as 'phonography' in 1837.

Despite living in the landlocked Cotswolds, former Campden Grammar School pupil Jonathan Hulls (died in 1758) grew up to be an inventor and is best known for his work in relation to the propulsion of vessels or ships using steam power.

The 'Dursley-Pedersen' bicycle was designed and developed by Danish inventor Mikael Pedersen (died in 1929) who came to live in Dursley in the 1890s bringing the concept with him and continuing to develop it thereafter.

For my money, however, Mr Bidmead of 'Leachlade' [*sic*] invented the most useful implement of all – his turnip cutter apparently put all others 'in the shade' for its 'simplicity, ease, expediency and cost'. An effusive newspaper report of 1856 describes the instrument as 'worked by a man with one hand', capable of cutting the full size turnip 'into small pieces at one blow', so continuing 'at each and as fast as the workman can rise and sink his arm' (*Wilts & Gloucestershire Standard*). Presumably, the only hitch might have been finding a one-handed man to work it.

8

VERY GRAVE

When it comes to fascinating epitaphs and monuments, the dedicated Cotswold church crawler is spoilt for choice. Incredible limestone chest tombs rank tall in mossy grandeur, extraordinary effigies stare out of the gloom of dark and ancient churches, and fine brasses abound, each telling the story of Cotswold life and death throughout the ages.

SOME MONUMENTAL MONUMENTS

St Kenelm's in Sapperton houses the impressive effigy of Sir Robert Atkyns (died in 1711). This notable gentleman was responsible for (among many other things) the weighty tome *The Ancient and Present State of Gloucestershire*, published the year after his death – still found buckling the shelves of most the county's libraries hereabouts. Inside Sapperton's beauteous light-infused church he grandly and permanently reclines in life-sized marble form with book to hand, courtesy of his wife, the Lady Louise.

The brightly painted effigy of Sir John Fortescue, former Lord Chief Justice and Lord High Chancellor (accompanied by a handsome blue-eyed lion), can be found at St Eadburgha's, Ebrington – a fortunate man if ever there was. As a staunch Lancastrian supporter, things were looking a tad grim for Sir John following the catastrophic Lancastrian defeat at Tewkesbury on 4 May 1471. Margaret of Anjou (queen consort of the mentally unstable Henry VI) escaped on the day of battle but was later deposited in the Tower of London, while Fortescue was pardoned and allowed to retire. His '*De Laudibus Legum Angliae*' was written for the instruction of Margaret and Henry's only son, Prince Edward, who wasn't quite so lucky. A brass plate at Tewkesbury Abbey marks the young prince's demise.

The church of St Andrew, Toddington, houses the most enormous monument to Charles Hanbury-Tracy, 1st Baron Sudeley, and his wife, Henrietta. Charles was Chairman of the Commission in charge of judging designs for the new Houses of Parliament, following the devastating fire of 1834. Nearby, his magnificent Gothic-style mansion, Toddington Manor (purchased by Damien Hirst in 2005), is currently being restored.

Among the Oxfordshire Cotswolds' most striking monuments are those of the once important Fettiplace family at St Mary's in Swinbrook. These two sets of three-man bunks have always put me in mind of exercise. Stick imaginary headphones on Sir Edmund junior (died in 1613), pa and grandpa below and it's hard not to think 'thigh crunch' (although admittedly, this might prove difficult to achieve dressed in armour). Sadly, for such a fit group of gents, the family line ran its course in the early 1800s and their posh house ended up in ruins.

St Bartholomew's in Notgrove is amply blessed with effigies – two ancient priest-like figures brought in from the churchyard and three members of the Whittington family in the form of two men and a beautifully dressed lady holding a book. Some 11 miles away, St Giles' in Coberley houses the tomb of Dick Whittington's mother.

Many of Painswick's superb limestone table tombs are attributed to local stonemason John Bryan. Mr Bryan's own tomb, however, is in a class all of its own – a pyramidal glory rising grandly from the Cotswold sod, ensuring that this fine craftsman will never be forgotten. Another excellent (smaller) pyramid stands in the old churchyard of St Mary's, Woodchester.

Impressive marble monuments figure at St James', Chipping Campden, including a particularly striking example featuring Edward Noel, Viscount Campden and his lovely wife, the Lady Juliana (died 1680) who stand barefoot behind open doors, both be-robed in shrouds and clasping hands. Their twenty-two-year-old daughter, the Hon. Penelope, 'over whose pretious dust' her parents sadly 'dropt theyr teares [*sic*]', describing her as 'the most exquisite model of nature's best workmanship', can be seen nearby. She is said to have died from blood poisoning, having pricked her finger while 'working with coloured silks'.

IT'S A FAMILY AFFAIR

The church of St Michael & All Angels in Withington houses a fascinating monument to Sir John Howe (died in 1670) and his wife, Bridgett, of Cassey Compton, gazing out from a lofty perch, with eight tiny children shown beneath.

Outdating and outnumbering the Howes by some measure is the Lloyd family of Ampney Crucis. Far away at the beautiful little church of the Holy Rood, former Lord of the Manor George Lloyd (cool moustache), his wife and twelve kneeling children (1584) lay undisturbed in the peace of this special place. The Lloyds' estate was eventually sold to the Pleydells, evidently a most fastidious family – their memorial tablets state the time of death as well as the date.

A representation of James Vaulx (died in 1626) resides at St Mary's in Meysey Hampton, along with his two wives – one each side. Head in hand, his elbow resting on a skull, it has to be said Vaulx looks pretty miserable – although, on reflection, perhaps just tired. His first spouse, Editha, is recorded as having 'lefte before her IX Sonnes and III Daughters, all of them the Pledges of that conjugall Love that was between herselfe and her surviving husband, who was That famous Practitioner in Physick and Chirurgery.'

A quirky monument installed by Edmund Harman (former barber/surgeon to King Henry VIII) at St John the Baptist in Burford shows his sixteen children kneeling in two separate panels – nine curly haired boys and seven girls.

'TIL DEATH US DO PART

A stone set into the floor at St Peter & St Paul's, Northleach, records that 'what was Mortal of Daniel and Eleanor Howes' lies 'underneath'. Mrs H died 6 August 1733, closely followed by Mr H on the 26th. It goes on:

In Life United in true conjugal Amity,
In Death but a short time Divided.

Another inseparable couple rests in the churchyard of St Lawrence's, Didmarton, where a poignant verse celebrates the love of 'T.M. 1759. M.M. 1759.':

Here lyeth two, whom death again hath wed
And made this grave their second marriage bed
Tho' death at first made some disconsolation
It could not make an utter separation.

Sir Thomas Smyth (died in 1593), his two wives and thirteen children are commemorated in stone at St James' in Chipping Campden along with a brass of William Gybbys, his three wives and thirteen little children. Mr Croston can be seen at St Mary's, Swinbrook with three wives, whilst another brass in the Trinity Chapel of St John Baptist, Cirencester, depicts Reginald Spycer (1442) with four diminutive wives, each modelling the must-have millinery of their day.

Thomas Williams (died in 1636) at Winchcombe seems to have been confident enough to leave a memorial space for his wife to join him in due course. His effigy depicts a big friendly (if somewhat irritating) face gazing across expectantly at where her image ought to kneel. I don't suppose he'd be too chuffed to know he's been alone on the shelf for over three centuries now – his relict apparently married somebody else.

Perhaps this Winchcombe William had the best deal of all. His spouse's epitaph at St Peter's simply reads:

She was - but words are
wanting to express
What She was,
think what a good Wife
ought to be:
and She was that.
Mary wife of William Best

THREE COLOURFUL CHARACTERS

It appears Lord Coleraine may have had a sensitive conscience. A marble memorial on the wall of St Mary's, Driffield reads:

Here lieth
In expectation of the last day
Gabriel Hanger, Lord Coleraine,
What manner of man he was
That day will discover
He died Jan 24 1773 Aged 75

Maybe the message was intended to serve as a warning to Lord Coleraine's youngest son George who, before his father's death, had already 'distinguished' himself while at Eton by what he describes, in his own words, as 'a most decided preference for female society', citing among his extra-curricular activities a carpenter's wife and the daughter of 'a vender of cabbages'. By the time he came of age, George had engaged in no less than three duels and married a gypsy – all vividly described in the rambling and extraordinary *Life, Adventures, and Opinions of Col. George Hanger. Written by Himself*. His epitaph admits that he 'was also a Practical Christian as far as his frail nature did allow him so to be'.

A memorial tablet at St George's in Nailsworth records that local architect Nathaniel Dyer (died in 1833) left means to pay the minister of Nailsworth Chapel to preach a sermon every sixth day of February (for one guinea). The chapel wardens got 10s and the remainder of the interest was 'to be distributed in bread to the Poor of Nailsworth for ever'. Despite paying for the plaque (£20) and designing the town's original 'Pepperpot Chapel' (built in 1793–4), you won't find this gentleman's grave in any cemetery. Nathaniel's plot of choice was rather closer to home. He was buried upright in a specially built mausoleum in his own orchard at Springhill House, Nailsworth, in an effort, so the story goes, to prevent his enemies from dancing on his remains. His will records instructions for each of his servants to receive 'a plain suit of mourning' and for the orchard to be entered each year (also on 6 of February) to make any repairs. A copy of an oil painting of Mr Dyer (and one of his four wives) hangs in his former residence, now a residential care home. He looks jolly enough.

Old Roger Rutter (alias Rudder) of Uley must surely be one of the Cotswolds' earliest recorded vegetarians. Situated close to the porch in the churchyard of St Giles' at Uley, his gravestone records that he was buried 30 August 1771 aged eighty-four years, 'Having never eaten Flesh, Fish, nor Fowl during/the Course of his long Life' – a diet that evidently served him well. According to tradition, this healthy gent lived principally on an uninspiring dish called 'dump' – a sort of dumpling made of suet – plain dump, hard dump, and, on particularly splendid days, apple dump. Roger's epitaph was inscribed by his grandsons. A memorial plaque to his son, Samuel (author of *A New History of Gloucestershire*, published 1779) can be seen at St John Baptist, Cirencester. Incidentally, it's just a whim, but I like to think R.R. was also partial to a slice of Heg Peg dump – a pudding or dumpling made of 'heg pegs' or 'ag pag' (wild plums) traditionally eaten at the nearby Nympsfield village feast.

An old local rhyme goes something like this:

> Nympsfield is a pretty place,
> Built upon a tump,
> And what the people live upon
> Is heg-peg dump.

ALL RATHER SUDDEN

Thomas Stone's stone (died in 1893) at St Bartholomew's in Notgrove, succinctly states that he 'departed this life (very suddenly)', as did Yeoman John Sansum (died in 1819), commemorated at St Mary's, Syde, who apparently 'went forth well' only to find Death 'sore surprized [*sic*]' him on the way – unlike his 'industrious Wife' Olive, who preceded her husband by 'slow degrees' six months earlier.

John Parker, aged fifty-six, of Painswick met an abrupt end on 4 September 1799.

As through the fields he walked alone,
    By chance he met grim Death:
Who with his dart, did strike his heart,
    And rob'd him of his breath.

Still, it could have been worse. One of his neighbours, Alice King (buried not far away), died the previous year on 11 June 1798, 'it being her Birth-day'.

TRADES & WARNINGS

A precise gravestone at Edgeworth states that Thomas Kight, aged seventy-two (died in 1867) was:

> For more than thirty five years and
> a half, the Coachman and faithful
> Servant of Edmund Hopkinson Esqre.
> Edgeworth Manor House

It then throws in a liberal dose of proverbs for good measure – 'Boast not thyself of tomorrow, for thou knowest not what a day may bring forth.'

The more reflective statement on the grave of Sarah Heath (died in 1888 aged eighty-six) at St Leonard's, Bledington, reads:

> Thou shalt come to thy grave
> in a full age like as
> a shock of
> corn cometh in in
> his season'

The same Bible verse appears on the grave of 104-year-old shepherd Richard Widdows at St Andrew's, Great Rollright.

Soap Boilers, a Felmonger and a mid-wife tell their tales at Cirencester. Sarah Avery's (died in 1833) stone reads:

Thirty seven years the Almighty gave me power,
To aid my sex in nature's trying hour,
Through heat and cold, by day and dreary night,
To save the hapless was my soul's delight.
Adieu

Meanwhile, William Lendon's (died in 1875) former trade is easy to discern. His grave at Slad reads:

My sledge and hammer are declined,
My bellows too has lost it's [*sic*] wind,
My fire's extinct, my forge decayed,
And in the dust my vice is laid;
My coal is burnt, my iron gone,
My springs at play, my work is done

TWO LASTING LEGACIES

A memorial to Viscount Lee of Fareham (died in 1947) can be found at Avening's Church of the Holy Cross. Lord Lee once lived at 'Old Quarries' in the village, which also served as a place of safekeeping for some of the artwork from the National Gallery during the Second World War. Among Lord Lee's many other services to his country was the donation of Chequers which he and his wife gave to the nation in 1921.

Not far away at the beautiful graveyard of Amberley's Holy Trinity Church is the final resting place of Major General Sir Fabian Ware (died in 1949), founder of the Commonwealth War Graves Commission. The Commission, established by Royal Charter in 1917, ensures a permanent, named, and uniform tribute to the men and women of the Commonwealth forces who paid the ultimate sacrifice in the two world wars.

FAR FROM HOME

A sad memorial at St Mary's in Woodchester tells the tale of twenty-seven-year-old 'Robert Paul Esqr., Commander of his Majesties Sloop, Pheasant', who died 'whilst cruising off Trinidad' in 1805:

Not feigned the sorrow, nor suborned the tear,
That pays due tribute to this early bier,
Each sailor wept, and each with misty eye,
For his loved captain heaved a parting sigh,
So mourned his friends too proud alas to claim,
A kindred interest in his rising fame;
For his firm breast the ocean had its charms,
The war of elements, the shock of arms,
And tho' no stone may mark his distant grave
On shores where rolls the transatlantic wave,
Here in this vale shall memory speak his praise
And fond affection here this tablet raise.

High up on the wall at St Mary Magdalene, Rodborough, a stone plaque with black and red lettering records the death of 'James Flight 12 years Engineer to the late Viceroy of Egypt', who died at Alexandria in March 1854. Somewhat curiously, the interest from his bequest of 'Forty-five pounds' is to be 'given to some poor person suffering from disease in the chest, at the recommendation of the Rector for the time being'.

The life-like bust of a nineteen-year-old man at St Peter's, Leckhampton, poignantly states:

Near Nazareth, Sepr. 14TH 1877.
William Joseph Gale,
Aged 19.
'He fell among robbers.'

TERRIBLY SAD

The empty chair of Augusta, 3rd Baroness Rossmore (died in 1840), depicted on her memorial at St Peter's, Stanway (not on view) speaks almost as eloquently as her husband's heart-rending entreaty:

> Who'eer thou art whose attention in passing by
> May be here attracted I pray you,
> To sympathize for a moment with him
> Who by his late bereavement feels like one,
> Who had lost his all in this world.

Amelia Jenkinson (died in 1770), first wife of Charles Jenkinson (later Earl of Liverpool), was also clearly too good for this world. Her sad epitaph at St Mary's, Hawkesbury, explains that she died 'from having given birth to her only child'. She was nineteen years old.

> Hence, adulation: to proud sculpture fly,
> Nor wound this honest marble with a lie;
> The truth, she lov'd, inscribes her gentle dust,
> Which almost blushes yet, at praise, tho' just.
> Of symmetry, the coldest breast to charm,
> Of modesty, to check a wish too warm;
> Of manners soft, by elegance refin'd,
> Nature's pure gift, with not an art combin'd:
> O'er ev'ry gesture, all she look'd or said,
> Propriety its happy influence shed;
> In her soft converse, cheerfully sedate,
> Joy assum'd wings, and grief forgot its weight:
> Superior to the world, in life's gay stage
> She liv'd, a heav'n-born pattern to the age.

A tablet close by records that her son, Sir Robert Bankes Jenkinson KG, 2nd Earl of Liverpool, served as Britain's Prime Minister for nearly fifteen years from 1812, following the assassination of Spencer Perceval KC in the lobby of the House of Commons.

HARD ACTS TO FOLLOW

Like ancient social network pages written in stone, the glowing characters and exemplary lives of our forebears make fascinating reading. Indeed, one can only wonder how the folk of Horton managed to go on without William Paston (1769) in their midst.

> A Mind enrich'd by Nature and by Art,
> With what could please and interest every Heart;
> In upper Life by all, who saw approv'd,
> In lower Life by all, who knew him, lov'd:
> No Epitaph his Virtues need proclaim,
> His Actions ever will indear his Name:
> An upright, Generous, open hearted Friend,
> HORTON! deplore thy Loss! lament his End!

The folk of Miserden are more pragmatic. 'Praises on tombs, / Are trifles vainly spent,' says the plate on Hannah Sheppard's tomb. 'A good name left, / Is a lasting monument'.

FOUR BIRDS, FOUR CATS...AND A GOAT

The most well-known dead cat in the region has to be Tiddles. Immortalised in stone next to the porch of St Mary the Virgin, Fairford, this moggie clearly appreciated a good sermon for it hung around the church for many years before passing on to cat heaven in 1980. Apparently, a Tiddles II has also recently frequented the churchyard and another devout puss, Tilly, stalks St Mary's churchyard at Painswick. According to a firm-sounding notice, he/she is not allowed to go inside the church, although I have it on good authority that this romantic roamer is particularly fond of weddings.

Feline fever increases over the county border at Malmesbury Abbey where a famous gravestone tells the bizarre tale of barmaid, Hannah Twynnoy, aged thirty-three, killed by a tiger in October 1703:

In bloom of Life
She's snatchd from hence,
She had not room
To make defence;
For Tyger fierce
Took Life away.
And here she Lies
In a bed of Clay,
Until the Resurrection Day.

The effigy of William Kingston (died in 1614) at St Andrew's in Miserden is accompanied by a goat said to be eating a cabbage (although it looks like he don't care for his greens to me) and a carved stone outside St Giles', Coberley, records the final resting place of trusty steed Lombard. Inside the church, a rare heart burial monument is thought to belong to Lombard's master, Sir Giles de Berkeley, who died away from home in the thirteenth century.

The remains of the affectionately dubbed 'bird lady of Avening' were discovered in an ancient stone coffin, accompanied by the skeletons of four small birds, during restoration work at the Church of the Holy Cross in the early 1900s and, whilst along this avian avenue, mention must be made of one of the many treats at St John the Evangelist, Elkstone – a stone spiral stairway leading to an amazing old dovecote with forty-three nest holes.

A NEAR MISS

The *Stroud Free Press* of January 1851 records the lucky escape of a bell-ringer at Cranham:

As a man named Probert was engaged with his brother bell ringers, in ringing the customary peel [*sic*] at the close of the old and commencement of the new year, he 'threw his bell' and went up into the bellfry [*sic*] in the dark to set it right, forgetting the other bells were in motion. He was struck down across the rafters where he must have remained for some minutes insensible, and been repeatedly struck about the head. Considerable hoemorrage [*sic*] took place, but his companions below, did not at first recognize [*sic*] that it was blood running through the ceiling. He was shortly removed to his own home, and Mr Gardner, of Painswick, called, who promptly attended the case, and found five or six inciser wounds upon the scalp, the nose cut, and arm bruised. The necessary measures were at once adopted, and the sufferer is now going on as favourably as can be expected.

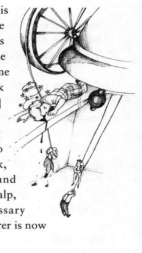

Still, if you have to depart, you might as well do it in style…

WHAT A WAY TO GO

The diary of John Osborne of Monk's Mill near Wotton-under-Edge notes the odd death of 'Mr Paston of Horton', recording that his demise came about as a result of 'a Needle & thread left in his Shirt by carelessness of a Servant, which in the night work'd itself into his Arm, caused an Inflamation [*sic*] and brought on a Mortification, owing to an extream [*sic*] bad habit of Body.' The same diarist writes of a Mrs Adey who 'in all probability' passed away in February 1769 as a result of 'eating too Great a quantity of Nutts & Filberds'.

The bizarre death of Martha Collins at King's Stanley in 1800 has long been remarked upon:

Twas as she tript from cask to cask,
In at a bung-hole quickly fell:
Suffocation was her task,
She had not time, to say farewel [*sic*].

Meanwhile, the tragic story of Lords Lisle and Berkeley and their bitter dispute over inheritance is woven into Cotswold history. To cut a long story short, these two guys gathered their supporters at Nibley Green on 20 March 1469/70 to have it out, although young Viscount Lisle didn't last long thanks to an impressive shot straight through his open visor by 'Black Will', an archer from the Forest of Dean. Leland writes that an arrow entered his mouth and passed out through his neck; another source reports that it pierced his left temple. In any case, he died.

No less ignominious was the plight of Elisabeth Chew from Bisley, who died nearly four centuries later in October 1857 having been knocked down by a donkey.

Finally, those that passed on during the reign of Charles II may have been dead but they certainly weren't cold – thanks to an exceedingly woolly law introduced to help boost trade. The act, passed in 1667 and finally repealed in 1814, decreed that 'no corpse of any person' (except those killed by the plague) should be 'buried in any shirt, shift, sheet or shroud or anything whatever made or mingled with flax, hemp, silk, hair, gold or silver or in any stuff or thing, other than what is made of sheep's wool only.' As if that wasn't onerous enough, an affidavit was also required to confirm that the law had been observed – the fine for transgression? A hefty £5. We'll give the very last word on the subject to poet John Oldham (born 1653 at Shipton Moyne):

I mind not the Members, and makers of laws:
Let them sit or prorogue, as His Majesty please;
Let them damn us to woollen, I'll never repine
At my lodging when dead, so alive I have wine…

9

BUT IT'S A TRADITION!

With the delights of PlayStation, Wii and the worldwide web at our fingertips, you might imagine such simple entertainments as rolling two Double Gloucester cheeses backwards round an old church to be 'old hat'. Surf the crazy Cotswolds, however, and you'll soon discover overwhelming evidence to the contrary, with many of the region's abundance of bizarre ancient traditions still very much alive and kicking. For example, each year thousands of spectators gather to watch competitors battle their way through the Cotswolds' own 'Olimpick' Games; others run uphill bearing 60lb sacks of wool on their backs, while folk who may not have darkened the door of a religious institution in years happily join hands to hug Mother Church – all with little sign of abatement.

FOOTBALL IN THE RIVER

There are some experiences in life you can't prepare for. The sight of twelve strapping Cotswold footballers gambolling about in the River Windrush is one of them. 'Football in the River' has been played at Bourton-on-the-Water for decades, but like all the very best traditions, the exact origin of the event remains something of a mystery – despite

a raft of fascinating evidence. There's an interesting wall painting of the game at the Old New Inn and another picture hangs in Victoria Hall. Old photographs and stories abound (not to mention bizarre recollections of an umbrella-wielding referee) and several Bourton folk still remember their fathers' river exploits from years ago.

This splashing showdown used to be a full-on competitive affair involving teams from other areas, until risk of player injury became cause for concern, especially when the grass banks were re-built in stone. So now it falls to opposing teams from Bourton Rovers Football Club to stage the aquatic activity every August Bank Holiday – the grand finale of a fun-packed fête.

At the strike of four, Bourton's cash tills fall silent and all sensible ducks take cover. Nets are placed between the bridges and the players solemnly don precautionary armbands before striking purposefully into the ankle-deep flow of the Windrush. A quick blow on the whistle, and they're off.

There follows thirty minutes of fast-flowing action as the lads take the beautiful game to water – not as easy as it looks, as several famous guest players have discovered. The trick comes in skilfully flicking the ball out of the water while making the most of the prevailing current – such watery wizardry provoking a series of involuntary guttural utterances from the crowd at the very slightest hint of a strike for goal, although it has to be said, the loudest screams have nothing whatsoever to do with the score. Rather, it's the mischievous Cotswold lads' merciless use of every tackling opportunity in the book to interact with their captive audience. Mums and dads, teens, grannies, Yorkshire terriers – none are safe from the sheets of icy cold Windrush water showering the banks, drenching everyone and everything in sight – not that anybody seems to mind. In the confusion no one's sure who's actually won, or even cares for that matter, as the crowds disperse after yet another fabulous Cotswold spectacle – much to the relief of local residents, Mr & Mrs M. Allard, who evidently consider the whole event, and everyone involved in it, 'absolutely quackers'.

BISLEY WELL DRESSING

Closeted deep in the heart of this idyllic place – cottage gardens rioting pink and blue; clucking hens scratching contentedly in the dust; spring exploding extravagantly in every hedgerow – the busy goings-on of the world seem far away as the children of Bisley lay down their delicate sacrifices of thanks for the life-giving water still springing forth in their village, as it has done for generations.

Bisley's Seven Wells are a handsome sight. Once the village's principal water supply, five Gothic canopies channel cascading water into a shallow semi-circular trough with two additional channels emerging at either end. To the right stand larger troughs originally used for washing purposes and for watering animals – although these days, it's pretty Ms Puddleduck and her friends who rule the roost.

Inscribed with the quote 'O ye wells bless ye the Lord praise Him and magnify Him for ever', along with the royal monogram commemorating the marriage of the Prince and Princess of Wales (later King Edward VII and Queen Alexandra), the current structures date from 1863, when the Revd Mr Thomas Keble restored the wells for the benefit of all. Keble was the incumbent of All Saints' Church from 1827 to 1873 and it was he who introduced the well-dressing occasion as a thanksgiving for Bisley's water.

The ceremony is still faithfully maintained by the Bisley Blue Coat Church of England Primary School, whose pupils play a major part in proceedings. Preparations for the event begin three days beforehand with the 'mossing-up' of special symbols, followed the next day by an afternoon of serious flower-power in the school playground, which is where, up to their eyes in petals, dedicated groups of parents, grandparents, children and villagers busily arrange the flowers into different shapes including two enormous stars of David, the letters 'AD', the numerals of the current year, the word 'Ascension' and a minimum of five small hoops. Care is taken to make sure everything conforms to the traditional pattern, even to the time of day.

After a brief service at All Saints' Church, the children prepare for the parade with all Year 6 attired in traditional nineteenth-century Blue Coat costume. As the Avening Silver Band strikes up, the clergy stand to attention, and the party proceeds down Bear Pitch, along the High Street and into Wells Road where, once assembled, the children divest themselves of their flowery burdens as the visiting speaker watches on from his watery perch aloft the Seven Wells. With hoops in position and every posy gently laid, the congregation joins in a hymn, after which the vicar duly gives the blessing.

Back at school, old pupils, visitors and villagers re-live the good old days as the Revd Mr Thomas Keble sleeps on in the churchyard next door. The 150th anniversary of the event will be celebrated in 2013.

THE RANDWICK WAP

Nobody in Randwick seems to bat an eyelid at the sight of three enormous Double Gloucester cheeses turning up at the local church each year. But then, 'Cheese Rolling Sunday' is as natural to a true 'Runnicker' as water to a duck, and as the bells ring out from St John's, the villagers flock in to celebrate their amazing, if not perplexing, ancient tradition.

Gathered outside round a mossy table-tomb, a hymn is sung and the Double Gloucesters duly blessed before, to delighted cries of 'Here it comes! The cheese is coming!', a horde of excited children finally get the chance to roll the cheeses widdershins (anti-clockwise) three times round the church.

Cheese Rolling Sunday is just part of a series of eccentric events on the Randwick calendar, starting in February with nominations for the offices of mayor (male or female) and queen and an election open to all villagers of eighteen and over who have signed the official Wap Poll Book. A high sheriff, sword bearer and 'mop man' are also appointed (from the runners-up) plus several other 'unofficial' additional roles including a flagman, cheese bearers, apprentices, princesses and ladies-in-waiting.

Results are revealed on 'Princess Saturday' in March by a town crier 'crying in' the lucky few destined to take the lead in a Wap ceremony, which villagers believe dates back to the Middle Ages – perhaps taking its present form as a celebration following the building of Randwick Church. Legend has it that an unfortunate hod man, having had one too many, found himself being 'refreshed' by his colleagues in the village pond. With its link to cheese-rolling and water, some believe the Wap to be related to Celtic pre-Christian fertility rites, while other sources suggest the word itself is derived from 'wappenshaw', describing a local weapons inspection.

Whatever its origins, the Randwick Wap is certainly synonymous with entertainment. One week on and the villagers throng round the war memorial to enthrone their mayor and Wap Queen on odd-looking chairs, while the town crier challenges anyone who knows of 'any just cause or impediment' why the incumbent should not be mayor, to declare themselves or forever hold their peace. And so the ceremony begins.

Conscious of his fate, it's likely Mr Mayor would actually quite welcome an interruption but, regrettably, no one seems inclined to challenge his office and so without further ado, his lordship is conscientiously drenched with spring water, hoisted aloft and, preceded by the infamous mop man and his apprentices assiduously mopping back the crowds, paraded downhill to Mayor's Pool, where he's promptly reversed into the water and mercilessly splashed yet again.

At last someone pipes up, 'Hadn't we better sing *the* hymn?' at which point, the old 'Mayor's Song' is struck up by a silver band (at the time of writing set to the tune of 'In Dulci Jubilo') and the crowd does its best to join in with:

> When Hercules began to spin
> Apollo wrought upon a loom;
> Our trade to flourish did begin
> Though conscience went to selling broom…

...and on and on for several other unfathomable verses before it's off to Well Leaze for more cheese rolling down a steep alleyway, followed by a jolly afternoon of fête festivity on the local playing fields accompanied, perhaps, by a delicious portion of Wiput (a milky dish traditionally eaten at the Wap). According to my source, today's recipe (passed down from the village elders) is 'slightly vague' although it's most likely some form of 'white pot', a bread pudding type concoction like this one:

> Two quarts of milk
> Six egg yolks and whites well beaten separately
> Three spoonfuls of fine flour stirred in by degrees
> Sweetened with treacle to taste
> Set over fire just to boil up
> Put in a pan and baked with bread.

I've also read that in days gone by, the dish was joked about as being enlivened by a tasty extra ingredient (closely related to Randwick's Lousey Stone, *see* page 29). Yum!

ONE BAG, TWO BAGS, THREE BAGS FULL

Once an important wool town, Tetbury is now better known for its most famous locals, The Prince of Wales and The Duchess of Cornwall – although it's highly unlikely you'll catch them donning their trainers for this curious Cotswold tradition! To the uninformed, Tetbury's Spring Bank Holiday event appears to be perfectly innocuous, the action beginning mid-morning with a colourful street fair featuring dancers, musicians, fire-eaters, exhibitions, open-air hospitality and dozens of stalls selling everything from fudge to flip-flops.

By one o'clock, however, things start to take a decidedly quirky turn as the crowds begin to migrate down Long Street in an effort to bag the best spot to witness doughty competitors of both sexes race up-and-down a breathtakingly steep hill, bearing ridiculously heavy sacks of wool on their backs.

The tricky slope in question is the curiously named Gumstool Hill – a tag that has stuck throughout the centuries since the days Tetbury had a ducking stool. It was also the site of the original woolsack races which are believed to date from the seventeenth century, when young drovers would show off to the fairer sex by racing up from the wool market at the bottom – the location of two happily placed public houses at either end of the hill perhaps having something to do with such ebullience. Not that the good folk of Tetbury encourage that kind of thing these days – there's no danger of being ducked any more either, for Tetbury's instrument of punishment is long gone – nor do you have to be a gossip, own a sheep, or even be a native to enter the races. You do, however, need to be fit, for Gumstool Hill is 1:4 in places – and that's not all.

With woolsacks (custom made by the British Wool Federation) weighing in at a hefty 60lb for men and 35lb for women, one might wonder why anyone would want to attempt the 240-yard feat. If recent years are anything to go by, however, there doesn't seem to be any lack of 'sacks with legs' disappearing down the slope only to be seen minutes later clawing back uphill – pain and determination etched on faces, as the crowds frantically egg competitors on to the finish.

Several celebrities have appeared at the event in recent years, including TV presenter Steve Backshall from CBBC's *Really Wild Show*, Olympic gold medal swimmer Sharron Davies MBE, Rory McGrath and Paddy McGuinness. Current world records (as at 2010) are:

Men's Teams: 2.53.09 (2003)
Men's Individual: 0.45.94 (2007)
Women's Teams: 4.08.35 (2005)
Women's Individual: 1.05.03 (2009)
Youth Teams: 2.51.00 (2006)

Most importantly, since the races were revived in 1973, hundreds of thousands of pounds have been raised for good causes. The Prince of Wales unveiled a plaque to mark the start line of the races on 25 May 1998.

PAINSWICK CLIPPING CEREMONY

The parishioners of Painswick near Stroud love their church. So much so, every year on Feast Sunday they join together en masse to show their appreciation at a charming 'clipping' ceremony. Many visitors wrongly imagine this must be something to do with St Mary's other claim to fame – its ninety-nine amazingly trim yew trees. What the Painswickians are really doing, however, is giving their dear old church the modern-day equivalent of a great big luvvie hug – traditionally observed on the Sunday of or first after 19 September, marking the dedication of the Church of the Blessed Virgin Mary.

The term 'clipping' is thought to derive from an old word meaning encircling or embracing, as in 'You elements that clip us round about!' (*Othello*) – used in this instance to describe the joining of hands to completely encircle or, as more simply conveyed to me by an elderly villager, 'to hug Mother Church in an expression of affection and gratitude'.

Formerly, the children of the parish, wearing floral headdresses and carrying posies, undertook the act of clipping, but these days adults are also allowed to join the fun. While the old custom is not unique to Painswick and is recorded in some other counties, St Mary's appears to be the only church in the Cotswolds with such a long-standing tradition – thanks to a much-loved former Painswick vicar, the Revd Mr William Herbert Seddon, who revived the event in September 1897. As to the custom's roots, things are not so certain – the Revd Mr Seddon suspecting it to be of 'Roman and Pagan' origin. Another source suggests that the joining of hands around the church in an ovate form relates to the representation in art of the Virgin Mary surrounded by a nimbus or glory.

Whatever its origins may be, today's event makes a pretty sight as following a rousing ring of bells, the choir and church leaders begin a solemn parade in the churchyard before everyone present is cordially invited to clip the church. A silver band then strikes up the hymn, 'Daily, Daily, Sing the Praises', as locals, tourists, ex-Painswickians, friends and strangers, young and old alike, join hands to step in and step out and give St Mary's a huge communal hug. In 2004 the current incumbent, the Revd Mr John Longuet-Higgins, introduced the additional act of facing outwards to clip the world as 'a sign of the church's commitment to faith sharing' – an innovation which remains in place today.

Following the clip, the visiting preacher receives advance wages – a basket of flowers and a bun – before mounting the narrow church tower steps to deliver a topical message. The children also receive a Painswick bun and a coin of the realm. Watch out if you get offered a slice of Puppy Dog Pie, though – a unique culinary treat traditionally dished up on Feast Sunday, along with a hilarious helping of local folklore. Versions abound of this wagging tale, but probably the funniest relates to a nineteenth-century landlady who cleverly dispensed with some troublesome navvies engaged in the construction of the Cheltenham to Bath turnpike, by serving them a dog meat pie. To this day, Painswick folk are known as Painswick Bow Wows. (Those of a squeamish nature may be relieved to know that Cotswold puppy dogs actually taste surprisingly like stewed fruit).

ROBERT DOVER'S OLIMPICK GAMES

Visit Chipping Campden on a certain evening in May and you'll find this characteristically tranquil Cotswold gem bursting with athleticism and energy, for this is when the locals gather at Dover's

Hill to try their luck at the Cotswolds' very own 'Olimpick' Games – an event which lays claim to being the first modern Olympic Games. The proceedings begin with the appearance, on horseback, of Robert Dover who, considering his famous games first came about in the 1600s, is wearing remarkably well. Resplendent in a crimson suit and fine feathered hat (courtesy of King James I), he rides across the hill to a temporary Dover's Castle accompanied by his patron, Endymion Porter, as the games officially open with a burst of cannon fire. The real Robert Dover, of course, died centuries ago, unlike his famous 'Olimpick' legacy, which, despite the interference of wars, laws, party-poopers and gate-crashers over the course of nearly 400 years, happily lives on to this day.

The original Dover's Meetings, boasting horse racing, field events, wrestling, coursing, and many other sporting activities, were a huge success, even drawing comparison with the original Greek Olympics as celebrated in *Annalia Dubrensia* (1636) – a collection of verse by leading poets of the time.

Apart from an interruption during the Civil War, they continued for nearly two centuries until 'disorder' allowed over-zealous nineteenth-century detractors to hasten their demise. The last games of that era took place in 1852, only to be re-kindled nearly 100 years later in 1951 – this time as part of the Festival of Britain – eventually leading to the formation, in 1965, of the Robert Dover's Games Society, under whose faithful care the games (celebrating their 400th anniversary in 2012) have remained ever since. According to their former honorary secretary, the late Dr Francis Burns, the use of the term 'Olimpick' has 'persisted over the centuries'. In 1988, the society received a British Olympic Association plaque and the BOA flag has been flown at all the games since 1996.

As to the format of today's event, the society works hard to keep a sense of the past while also responding to the interests of the present. One old-time crowd-puller guaranteed never to go out of fashion, however, is the spectacle of shin kicking, which dates back to the original Jacobean Games. Contestants dressed in white coats (representing shepherd's smocks) hold each other by the shoulder while attempting to weaken their opponent's legs by kicking their

shins – the object of the exercise being to get your opponent on his back (while he's unbalanced taking evasive action – or from the pain) – with a throw. (Thankfully, today's competitors are allowed to protect themselves by stuffing straw down their boots.)

Elsewhere, other fit individuals wield sledgehammers and take part in 'spurning the barre' in their attempt to win the coveted accolade of 'Championship of the Hill', while still more athletes set off on a 5-mile run and local pub teams battle it out in feisty tug-of-war challenges.

The lighting of an enormous bonfire and streams of coloured rockets signal the end of the games, but not before one final marathon treat as down in the waiting streets of Campden, faint echoes of pipes and drums announce the imminent torch-lit arrival of a whole community progressing down from the hill, ready to dance the night away.

Next afternoon, they're all back in The Square for Campden's Scuttlebrook Wake, another traditional community event featuring Maypole dancing and the crowning of a new Scuttlebrook Queen before, with visitors melting back to its charming shops and tearooms, the serene and abidingly beautiful Chipping Campden resumes its soporific calm as if nothing at all has happened.

WOODSTOCK MOCK-MAYOR DAY

The continued annual observance of an old mayor-making tradition held on the edge of the Oxfordshire Cotswolds at Woodstock, in which a mock mayor, corporation and officers are elected with mock formality before receiving their comeuppance in the River Glyme, is just as mad as it sounds.

Although geographically adjacent, Old Woodstock was independent of the borough of New Woodstock until 1886, and it's thought the original ceremony may have been a light-hearted send-up of the borough authority and its new town hall, completed in 1776, just ten years prior to the first recorded date of the event. Billed as 'one of the oldest and funniest' events in Oxfordshire, today's shenanigans begin with the outgoing corporation (impressively turned out in an assortment of bowler hats, Oxford University gowns and mortarboards) clambering aboard an open-sided lorry parked up at the local pub, in order to present their manifestos before a rowdy crowd. Inducements can be anything from promising to erect strategically positioned toll-gates allowing Old Woodstock residents exemption from the council tax, to proposals of a Woodstock high-speed car race, before, amid much heckling from the floor, the town crier announces that the corporation is ready to 'go into conclave'. With that, a plastic curtain is drawn over proceedings as, with muffled mutterings of 'I'll second that', 'All those in favour' and 'Aye, Aye', the voting gets underway.

Previous esteemed mock mayors include several Woodstock ladies and even actor Chris Chittell (aka Eric Pollard from the popular British soap opera *Emmerdale*). On election, the new mock mayor is duly attired in a red nineteenth-century Witney blanket, a chain of office made from assorted bits of metal and curtain rings and a splendid old top hat from Dunn & Co of Piccadilly. There follows a brief photo opportunity in the pub car park from whence Old Woodstock's new mock mayor and his ecstatic supporters process on a picturesque jaunt (courtesy of the Duke of Marlborough) via the stupendous beauty of Blenheim Park.

Back out through the Town Gate and it's straight up to the Town Hall where, in a recent addition to tradition, Woodstock's 'real' town mayor waits to receive his/her rival and the two are seated next to one another. Following scenes of vociferous approval from his team, it's time for the mock mayor and his officers to brush the dust off their feet, as they metaphorically turn their backs on authority and prepare to return to Old Woodstock via the natural boundary line of the River Glyme.

Once there, the mock mayor is stripped of his glad rags and unceremoniously chucked into the chilly flow, followed closely by his crazy colleagues as they make a dignified, if soggy, retreat to the pseudo-sanity of the Black Prince bar. As with many of today's delightful Cotswold traditions, this event continues to raise significant sums for local good causes.

CHEESE ROLLING AT COOPER'S HILL

Perched aloft the precipice of Cooper's Hill near Brockworth as the master of ceremonies bellows out, 'One to be ready, two to be steady, three to prepare and four to be off!', it's hard to imagine anything more madcap than attempting to chase a Double Gloucester cheese down its 1:2 (1:1 in places) incline. No matter how fit, it's almost impossible for any competitor to stay upright for more than a few bounds and yet, despite untold tales of terrible tumbles and punctured pride, this seemingly addictive annual pastime draws all manner of would-be heroes from all over the world. A 'rebel' cheese rolling took place in 2011 following the cancellation of the 'official' event for a second year running.

DUCK RACING AT BIBURY

The Downs above Bibury were once known for the famous Bibury Club horse race meetings, although these days the villagers of Bibury much prefer to race...um...ducks. Introduced to raise funds for the Bibury Cricket Club about twenty-five years ago, the event is rapidly becoming a new Cotswold tradition as up to 1,000 hardy visitors turn out every Boxing Day morning to cheer on some 3,000 yellow ducks (of the plastic variety) as they bob their way down the chilly Coln. The winner gets a cash prize, while the owner of the final quacker across the line takes home an oven-ready cousin. A second race, involving approximately 150 life-size decoy mallards, is also held with proceeds going to the charity of the winner's choice. The Bibury Cricket Club badge features three ducks – naturally. Meanwhile, the Bibury Cup race is still held every June at Salisbury Racecourse.

THE COTSWOLD MORRIS

Morris dancing has a long history in the region with many of today's teams still dancing from the 'Cotswold Style' collected (and later published) by the likes of Cecil Sharp (died in 1924), whose famous chance encounter with the Headington Quarry Morris Dancers on Boxing Day 1899 is now part of folklore itself.

The dances from a village are known as 'a tradition' – approximately twenty traditions have survived with Cotswold dances now enjoyed by hundreds of modern-day revival sides all over the world. A typical side is made up of six dancers accompanied by one or more musicians (traditionally, the pipe and tabor consisting of a three-holed whistle and a small drum). The Squire is the boss, the Fool frolics around with a pig's bladder on a stick amusing the crowd, the Foreman is the dance expert/teacher, the Bagman performs the role of secretary and, finally, some sides sport a 'beast of disguise'.

Many a Cotswold side can be observed, along with dozens of other Morris dancers, a-capering atop Gloucestershire's May Hill on May Day to dance in the dawn. A similar event is held on Painswick Beacon. Thereafter the sides 'dance out' throughout the summer months at all kinds of events, both home and abroad. The Morris is also well represented on Boxing Day outside the Cathedral at Gloucester where the City of Gloucester Mummers perform their traditional mummers' play each year.

Ten old Cotswold dances still performed
Balance the Straw – from various villages including Leafield and Bledington
Bean Setting – from Headington Quarry
Constant Billy – most Cotswold sides dance a version
Idbury Hill – from Bledington
Laudnum Bunches – from Headington Quarry
Princess Royal – a dance found in many Cotswold villages
Trunkles – a dance found in many Cotswold villages
Young Collins – versions collected in Longborough, Oddington and other places
Shepherds Hey – most Cotswold villages had a dance to this tune
Orange in Bloom – from Sherborne

Just fifteen of the twenty-first century sides performing in the Cotswolds
Abingdon Morris
Adderbury Morris (two sides)
Bampton Morris (three sides)
Chipping Campden Morris Men
Ducklington Morris
England's Glory Ladies Morris
Eynsham Morris
Gloucestershire Morris Men
Headington Quarry Morris Men
Ilmington Morris Men
Kirtlington Morris
Lassington Oak Morris Men, Highnam near Gloucester
Ragged and Old, Bussage
Stroud Morris Dancers
Oxford City

10

ON THIS
COTSWOLD DAY

1 January 1910
The rapid approach of the so-called Daylight Comet prompted
'Madge of Truth' of the *Evesham Journal & Four Shires Advertiser*
to reflect on the 'enormous admiration for astronomers' the story
engendered – not to mention 'tolerance for the peculiarities which
some of them display[ed]'. 'Their wives and daughters', it was
observed, 'would allow for any shortcomings at the breakfast table
for instance'.

5 January 1940
A detached Cotswold country cottage with three bedrooms and a
large garden was advertised for £400.

5 January 1962
A detached Cotswold country cottage with half an acre of garden was
advertised for £1,800.

5 January 2006
A semi-detached Cotswold country cottage with no garden was
advertised for £325,000.

7 January 1643
Prince Rupert attempted, unsuccessfully, to take Cirencester during
the first Civil War.

10 January 1840
Rowland Hill's Uniform Penny Post came into operation across the
country – one local newspaper cautiously observed that 'time alone
will determine its advantages whatever they may be.' Incidentally, this
is not the same (Revd Mr) Rowland Hill commemorated at Wotton-
under-Edge by a row of almshouses – often confused with Sir Ro.

That said, the town does have a postal pedigree – a highly prized cancellation stamp unique to Wotton. A Penny Black featuring the stamp was sold in 1988 for £30,800.

25 January 1858

The Princess Victoria, Princess Royal married Prince Frederick William of Prussia at St James' Palace, London. Amid reports of Gloucester's lavish celebration plans (including a Russian gun drawn by six horses, dinners for the poor, a mayoral banquet and a grand ball), Stroud's committee of management were determined that Stroud 'shall not be left behind'. Their 'display of loyalty' comprised an illumination of the Subscription Rooms 'on a scale of brilliance never yet seen in our town', four 3ft letters 'PR' and 'PP' formed of variegated oil lamps and, naturally, a grand ball. Despite only 120 people turning up to said ball, this 'charmingly select, perfectly harmonious' event proved an unqualified success with dancing until dawn. The royal bride and her husband were toasted three times three and a great many cheers more shook the very building (*Stroud Free Press*).

29 January 1868

William Bird, chimneysweep, was arrested for being drunk in Cirencester marketplace having knocked on the door (still dressed in his sooty clothes) of a Mr Baily, at 11.30 p.m., wanting a ticket for the hunt ball. Mr Bird later protested that he offered a sovereign for a ticket but Mr Baily knocked the money out of his hand. Verdict: no ticket and a five bob 'stay in your place' fine.

1 February 1856

Initial peace terms were negotiated to end the Crimean War. Nailsworth's rejoicings included a royal twenty-one-gun salute fired in 10½ minutes from its two cannon. Despite the existence of a narrow passageway called Gun Barrel Alley, there aren't any cannons in Nailsworth these days. However, they were clearly still around in 1892 when the new parish of Nailsworth came into existence on 26 March and both were fired within seconds of the midnight hour.

2 February 1643
Prince Rupert stormed Cirencester again, this time taking 1,200 prisoners and killing over 300 in just a few hours.

2 February 1856
The *Wilts & Gloucestershire Standard* reported that residents of Lechlade were baulking at paying 9*d* for a 4lb loaf when the same bread was being sold at Faringdon and Kempsford for 8½*d*. A century and a half later and the dough is still rising. A Cotswold baker hits national headlines for charging £21 for his 2-kilo mail-order loaf (including postage).

4 February 1851
A public meeting was held at Stroud Subscription Rooms to 'consider the propriety of adopting a Petition to Parliament, praying the Total and Immediate repeal of the window tax', while the *Stroud Free Press* joined a general call across the country for change, declaring England to be 'the highest taxed country in the world' with 'none of its taxes more obnoxious than that imposed upon us for the enjoyment of the light of heaven.' The tax was eventually repealed in July 1851 having been levied in England since 1697.

9 February 1767
A letter to the *Gloucester Journal* detailed the tragic and painful death of two young sisters and a maid servant at Coates, accidentally poisoned by 'arsenick' [*sic*] sold to the family as 'cream of tartar' by a quack.

1 March 1861
The Bourton-on-the-Water and Cotswold Village Hospital was

established – one of the first village hospitals in England. A regular newspaper report of its progress in the late 1800s revealed that fifty-nine out-patients were seen in June 1892. Patients admitted numbered six, and six were discharged. Support from the community included 2½ brace of trout, two dozen eggs, some old linen and a chair.

3 March 1542

Despite being declared innocent, Lord of the Manor of Painswick, Arthur Viscount Lisle, seemed determined to die in the Tower of London, where he was being held on suspicion of involvement in a plot. Shortly after receiving news of his restoration to favour, he expired from excitement.

4 March 1947

Continuing arctic weather across the country resulted in the closure of every single main road in the Gloucestershire County Surveyor's Cotswold division for many days. Such was the severity of conditions that ploughing was impossible and drifts had to be cut out by hand. Tons of ash and grit were used throughout the county, with prisoners of war being drafted in to help with the effort.

21 March 1646

The last major battle of the first Civil War was fought near Stow-on-the-Wold. Outmanoeuvred, Sir Jacob Astley's Royalist troops fought on into The Square but defeat was inevitable. Those not killed were captured and held prisoner in the church. A plaque outside St Edward's commemorates the event along with the memorial of Royalist officer Hastings Keyt of Ebrington inside. One of the cannon balls from the battle is held at the Corinium Museum, Cirencester.

1 April 1858

Harriet Gardner and Caroline Hunt caused a spectacle at a shop in Bisley in a dispute over three pence. A newspaper article of the day sarcastically reported their tongues going 'for a long time with that speed for which the sex is proverbial' before a 'set-to' involving the planting of blows, the pulling of hair, and the scratching of faces, all 'in the style peculiar to female pugilism'. Harriet Gardner was summoned for assault but the case was dismissed (*Stroud Free Press*).

12 April 1856

The local press reported on a luggage train derailment at Brimscombe station, resulting in several carriages pitching down a steep embankment. Among the cargo, a cask of gin (above proof) rolled down the slope leaking its contents on to the road whereupon 'a number of bargemen, navvies, laboring [*sic*] men and others' eagerly availed themselves of 'the fiery beverage, lying on their stomachs and lapping it from the ground'. Several ended up staying there, 'unable to move' (*Wilts & Gloucestershire Standard And Cirencester and Swindon Express*).

14 April 1556

Lord of the Manor of Painswick, Sir Anthony Kingston, died at Cirencester on his way for trial in the capital, for suspected conspiracy. It is unlikely Cotswoldians shed any tears for his particularly evil life.

15 April 1912

The RMS *Titanic* passenger liner sank on her maiden voyage across the Atlantic having struck an iceberg. Among the 1,517 that lost their lives was the American-born artist Francis Davis

Millet – one of the 'Broadway Colony' of artists in the Cotswolds. A lych-gate with Latin inscription in his memory can be found at St Eadburgha's, Broadway.

23 April 1661
Charles II was crowned at Westminster Abbey. Over two centuries later, a grand purple 'chair of state' intended for the Archbishop of Canterbury, who officiated at the ceremony, became the subject of an unusual bequest to the cottage hospital at Moreton-in-Marsh, having passed through the hands of several owners over the years before ending up with a Dr Sands Cox. Mistakenly believed to have been associated with the trial and execution of Charles I, 'The Juxon Chair', along with its accompanying footstool, remained on show at the hospital until 1928 before being sold to the Victoria and Albert Museum, where it can still be seen – British Galleries, Room 56d, Case 9.

24 April 1786
The *Gloucester Journal* recorded the death of Ann Davis of Tetbury at the age of 'upwards of 102', stating she had 'the perfect use of her faculties till the last minute – although this is debatable. Apparently, the old girl hadn't ventured out of her room for thirty years, 'nor ever during that time, even in the most extreme severe weather, would suffer any fire in her chamber.' Perhaps she was trying to compete with another Tetbury parishioner, Henry West, whose incredible record of Cotswold longevity during the 1600s beggars belief. According to the history books, he lived to the grand old age of 152, had ten children (by his fifth wife) and saw 100 grandchildren, to each of whom (for reasons probably best known to himself) he gave a pot or kettle made out of bell metal.

3 May 1951
The Festival of Britain officially opened in London. The Cotswolds' own Laurie Lee was Curator of Eccentricities and Chief Caption Writer, for which he was later appointed MBE.

8 May 1945 (VE-Day)
Along with the rest of the country, Cotswoldians enjoyed a 'brief period of rejoicing' (Churchill) including the villagers of Southrop, who assembled in the school to hear the Prime Minister's broadcast,

before forming a procession made up of children with musical instruments, bicycles, babies in decorated prams, and go-carts – not forgetting a 'very woe-begone Hitler bringing up the rear'. Siddington parishioners attired themselves in fancy dress and headed (with the accompaniment of 'rollicking music') for the Greyhound Inn to take up the landlord's generous offer of a thirty-six of beer and a ten of cider with two gallons of milk for the children (well, it would have been rude not to, wouldn't it?), while members of the Royal Air Force played football matches with the villagers of Ablington and Bibury (losing both) and the folk of Elkstone laid on 'a splendid tea', the high spot of which was an iced and decorated victory cake. (*Wilts & Gloucestershire Standard And Cirencester and Swindon Express*).

31 May 1902

A peace treaty was signed signalling the end of the second Anglo-Boer War. News reached Moreton-in-Marsh at an early hour with detonators and fog signals being let off at the railway station. By 11 a.m., Northleach was be-flagged with children parading the town, cheering and performing on 'unmusical instruments', while Chipping Campden indulged in a spot of Maypole dancing and a demonstration of Indian club swinging. Intermittent explosions of gunpowder from a late-night bonfire in the Market Square at Stow made sleep 'well-nigh impossible', while at Winchcombe, an effigy of ex-president Kruger was carried shoulder-high, followed by a series of speeches at Abbey Square. The Women's Institute at Upper Slaughter marked the occasion with 'the making of a handsome iced cake and a competition for a vase of flowers' (*Evesham Journal & Four Shires Advertiser*).

31 May 1858

Preparations to fire a Russian trophy gun presented to Cirencester following the Crimean War were scuppered by the steward and bailiff of the town, who secured the services of a blacksmith to 'spike' it the night before. Public indignation was 'intense'. The event committee decided to put the gun in mourning by decorating it with black crape, following which the cannon was horse-drawn round the town escorted by (among many others) the Band of the Royal North Gloucester Militia, the Independent Order of Odd Fellows, the Bear Club, the Black Horse Club, the Nags Head Club and the Ancient Order of Foresters.

1 June 1533
Anne Boleyn was crowned Queen of England at Westminster Abbey.
A subsequent royal tour with Henry in 1535 included such places as
Winchcombe, Sudeley, Leonard Stanley and Little Sodbury.

18 June 1815
Napoleon Bonaparte was defeated at the Battle of Waterloo.
Cotswold celebrations included country dancing and a strolling
band of musicians at Campden (where a recruiting sergeant present
distinguished himself by securing fourteen recruits, along with a bride)
while over at Nailsworth, residents erected a massive peace pole at the
Cross, which finally blew down during a gale in January 1839.

18 June 1979
A project to drill for oil began at Guiting Power. Despite drilling to a
depth of 6,500ft, no oil was found.

24 June 1902
Edward VII went down with appendicitis, seriously disrupting
the country's celebration plans for his coronation scheduled for
26 June. Following news that he was out of immediate danger, the
Chairman of the Bonfires issued a press appeal for the ignition of
coronation fires to go ahead. Cotswoldians obligingly responded but,
unfortunately, a heavy rain set in which interfered with the spectacle.
Within twenty-five minutes of lighting the fire at Chipping Norton,
an unplanned blaze broke out at a nearby licensed victualler's,
necessitating the services of the town's new steam engine, *King
Edward*. Unfortunately, residents' disappointment had earlier got the
better of some at Stow, prompting 'expressions of hostility' to be made
outside the residences of various Coronation Committee members
and the surreptitious lighting of the coronation bonfire. One can only
hope the 'aged and infirm poor' of Northleach got their promised gift
of beef and plum pudding.

26 June 1742
The Revd Mr John Wesley preached from a butcher's block in The
Shambles at Stroud.

8 July 1822

> Thus solemnized and softened, death is mild
> And terrorless as this serenest night

A storm at sea claimed the life of the English poet Percy Bysshe Shelley – his final moments sadly a far cry from the sentiments expressed in his poem, 'A Summer Evening Churchyard, Lechlade'. A plaque at Shelley's Walk close to the church of St Lawrence commemorates the poem's composition at Lechlade.

2 July 1859

A Penny Bank opened in Cirencester. Almost 250 Cotswold folk 'of all ages and classes' turned up long before opening time to 'avail themselves' of its advantages, depositing £8, 13s and 2d in sums varying from 10s to 1d (*Wilts & Gloucestershire Standard*).

10 July 1940

The German Luftwaffe launched its first attack in what became known as the Battle of Britain. A plaque at Northleach records that 'Fighter Pilots of No. 87 Squadron Royal Air Force' were billeted at the town's Walton House during this time. A stone memorial at Windrush is dedicated 'to the memory of Sgt Pilot Bruce Hancock RAFVR who sacrificed his life by ramming and destroying an enemy Heinkel bomber while flying an unarmed training aircraft from Windrush Landing Ground during the Battle of Britain on 18 August 1940'.

10 July 1553

Young Lady Jane Grey was proclaimed Queen of England – but only for nine days. She was beheaded for high treason at Tower Green, London, on 12 February 1554, far away from the Cotswolds where she'd briefly lived at Sudeley Castle, near Winchcombe, as ward of King Henry VIII's widow, Katherine Parr. The Lady Jane also served as chief mourner at the former Dowager Queen's funeral at the castle in 1548.

24 July 1822

Mary Conell was convicted for selling peppermint water in Tetbury without a licence.

6 August 1892

An advertisement in *Wilts & Gloucestershire Standard* recommended 'Towle's Pennyroyal and Steel Pills for females' for the speedy correction of all irregularities, removal of obstructions, and relief from 'the distressing symptoms so prevalent with the sex'.

13 August 1892

An advertisement in the local press claimed that Sunlight Soap 'will make a man look well, feel well and show the world that his laundress is up with the times' – assuming she's remembered to take her Steel Pills, of course (*Wilts & Gloucestershire Standard*).

14 August 1909

Aviation pioneer Samuel Franklin Cody took his first passenger on a flight. Shortly afterwards, Mrs Cody became the first woman to fly in Britain, prompting the aforementioned 'Madge of Truth' to offer her female readers some pre-emptive advice on 'what to wear when flying' – low-heeled boots, puttees and 'almost tight-fitting knickerbockers', apparently. No doubt, Mr Cody would have really hit it off with Brother Eilmer, the famous 'Flying Monk of Malmesbury', who launched himself from a tower in AD 1010 wearing wings attached to his hands and feet. Eilmer managed to stay airborne for approximately 200 metres before busting both legs on his return to terra firma. The 1,000th anniversary of his epic leap of faith was marked at Malmesbury in December 2010.

14 August 1800

The boss of Woodchester Mill treated his staff to one whole Buffalo and two hogshead of beer to celebrate the anniversary of a visit by King George III and Queen Charlotte (accompanied by their three eldest daughters, the Princess Royal and Princesses Augusta and

Elizabeth) in 1788. It's hard to imagine the workers had much of an appetite. One of their colleagues, Joseph Stephens, was due to face the gallows two days later.

24 August 1682

The Bishop of Gloucester wrote to the Archbishop of Canterbury to report a serious event at Barington [*sic*] church, where in a 'fitt of drunkenesse' Lord Wharton's son and others had entered the church at night, 'rent' the bible, rung the bells backwards and damaged the desk of the pulpit. Following 'tender expressions' of regret, the culprits handed over a sum of 40 guineas towards much needed repairs at St Edward's, Stow-on-the-Wold, and the bishop wisely offered his Grace a 'Lamprey Pye'.

2 September 1592

Elizabeth I visited Cirencester during her summer progress and was presented with a 'fayre cuppe of dowble gilt' along with an 'oration made in Latyn'.

2 September 1666

The Great Fire of London began at a baker's in the early hours, eventually destroying eighty-seven churches and many thousands of homes and buildings. Cotswold masons played their part in the reconstruction of the devastated city, including Edward and Thomas Strong, whose work is commemorated on a memorial near Sir Christopher Wren's grave in the crypt of St Paul's Cathedral:

> Remember the men who
> Made shapely the stones
> Of Saint Pauls Cathedral
> 1675–1708
> Edward Strong. Thomas Strong
> And all who laboured with them
> This tablet was erected by
> The Worshipful Company of Masons

Another famous Cotswold mason (who also worked on St Paul's), Christopher Kempster, is commemorated at St John the Baptist, Burford. Kempster's Day Book and a transcript are displayed at the town's Tolsey Museum.

3 September 1939

Prime Minister Neville Chamberlain announced that Britain was at war with Germany. A local paper quoted the comments of one member of a regiment stationed near London – 'God only knows where it will all end' – describing London as 'macabre' and 'grim' with people 'moving about like ghosts' in an 'inky blackness'. Elsewhere in the paper, a Cotswold vicar encouraged everyone to be more regular and frequent in their church attendance, arguing, 'our religion helps us to keep a sane, a clean, and a cheerful outlook on life' (*Wilts & Gloucestershire Standard*).

12 September 1840

The ladies of the Cotswolds were advised that among the most elegant of the season's carriage bonnets were those composed of a new type of fancy straw, lined with a white kind of 'gros d'Afrique', trimmed with white ribbons and ostrich feathers. Thought to be the largest bonnets of the season, the curtain at the back of the crown (composed of white silk) was warned against as 'excessively' and 'unbecomingly' deep. Fast forward to September 1929 and it was 'rubberised coats of fancy, velvet, very gay and bright', which were all the rage – those in 'pheasant colouring' being considered 'extraordinarily smart' (*Evesham Journal & Four Shires Advertiser*).

21 September 1815

Sarah Vevers of Horsley was committed to Horsley House of Correction, awaiting trial for 'being an incorrigible rogue and possessing ends of woollen yarn without satisfactory explanation' (Gloucester Records Series, vol. 22).

7 October 1782

Church officials at Bourton-on-the-Water decided to go to a Justice to get a warrant for Thos. Gardiner 'not paying for his Bastard by Eliz. Coats' (transcription of Vestry minutes).

8 October 1782

Thos. Gardiner caused further vexation by only being able to pay £2 2s of his £5 4s debt, so a large brass brewing kettle weighing 35lbs was taken by way of security (transcription of Vestry minutes).

9 October 1476

King Edward IV signed a charter granting Richard the Abbot of Evesham 'for ever, to have yearly two fairs to be held and kept within the Borough aforesaid, on two feasts of the year', Saints Philip and James, and 'the feast of the Translation of Saint Edward, King and Confessor'. Stow's excellent position in relation to some important trade routes made it the ideal location for business – the narrow alleyways, or 'tures', like the one between the Talbot and the pharmacy in Stow's Square thought to have been used for channelling the many thousands of sheep sold there. In later years, Stow Fair became more famous for horse dealing, with hundreds of farmers, traders and gypsies flocking to the town from all over the country – an event still observed today (albeit on a smaller scale) by the gypsy community, which continues to gather twice yearly on the nearest Thursdays to 12 May and 24 October.

10 October 1851

In a curious 'rags to riches' story, the passing of Mr Thomas Hale, aged seventy-eight, a poor and illiterate farmer from Greet near Winchcombe, made local news. By the time of his death he had amassed £100,000 – a staggering sum for the time. Between £10,000 and £20,000 in cash was found at his house. 'Such was his love for shining metal' reported the paper, 'he turned bank notes into gold.' It seems at some point his prospects had mysteriously undergone a dramatic change thanks to a considerable sum bequeathed to him by some 'maiden ladies' (*Stroud Free Press*).

14 October 1782

Thos. Gardiner was given notice to 'remove to his own Parish or prevent his wife from pulling hedges'.

24 October 1785

The *Gloucester Journal* excitedly reported that Signor Rossignoll, whose astonishing performance (involving a grand imitation of various birds in his throat) had been honoured with the approbation of the King, Queen and royal family, was to stop off at Stroud, Tetbury and Malmesbury on his way to London, performing two nights in each town.

2 November 1929

A local newspaper announced 'The Talkies Are Coming', offering its readers the chance to 'See and Hear the Greatest Singing and Talking Triumph' – in the form of *The Singing Fool* starring Al

Jolson – further adding that 'the 'talkie' projectors were among the mechanical marvels of the age and only an advanced technician could appreciate their wonders to the full.' Unfortunately, 'unforeseen difficulties' made it necessary to postpone the viewing until a later date (*Wilts & Gloucestershire Standard*).

5 November 1605
A plot to blow up the Houses of Parliament in London was foiled. Mr Johnson (aka Guy Fawkes) was arrested beneath the building in the early hours. A room at the manor of Lypiatt Park, near the Cotswold village of Bisley, is traditionally said have been used by the conspirators.

18 November 1852
The state funeral of the Duke of Wellington took place in London. A number of shops in the Stroud area closed as a mark of respect – much to the chagrin of many customers from the country who found themselves 'exposed to and suffering considerable disappointment', several being compelled to return 'a distance of upwards of seven miles without transacting their business' (*Stroud Free Press*).

26/27 November 1703
The Great Storm hit Britain, causing widespread devastation. Three of Fairford's famous stained-glass windows suffered serious damage – ironically, one of them featuring the Last Judgement. That same year, lightning struck Little Sodbury Manor for a second time – a poignant reminder of the tragic occasion in 1556 when lightning entered the parlour door, resulting in the death of the Lord of the Manor, Maurice Walsh, and seven of his children.

30 November 1887
A cow being driven past Stroud's Sun Dial Inn, 'perhaps having a thirst for the liquors so prominently advertised outside', walked up to the pub's door (conveniently open presumably), along the passageway and into the bar. No doubt the farmer was not far behind (*Stroud Journal*). The building, now a private dwelling, still sports a dial.

11 December 1936
King Edward VIII broadcast the news of his abdication to the nation. Local dignitaries and several hundred townsfolk gathered to signify

their allegiance to King George VI at a special ceremony in the Cirencester market place three days later – an occasion marred by 'the worst possible weather conditions', as a gale blowing throughout the morning reached its height and 'roar[ed] round the parish church tower', accompanied by torrential rain (*Wilts & Gloucestershire Standard*).

Christmas Eve 1539
The ancient abbey at Hailes was dissolved, its famous pilgrim-pulling relic, a phial of 'Christ's blood', turning out to be nothing more than coloured gum or honey. What little remains (apart from those bits 'absorbed' into several other buildings about the Cotswolds) stands defiantly opposite the tiny church at Hailes, near Winchcombe.

Christmas Day, Sunday 1836
Heavy snows lasting a whole week commenced at noon just as Cotswold folk were coming out of church, while the Duke of Wellington (still alive at this point and travelling in a carriage with outriders between Marlborough and Badminton) found the roads impassable. Royally inconvenienced, the poor old Iron Duke had to put up for the night at a local inn.

27 December 1890
Highly recommended as a 'never-failing and permanent cure' for 'Scrofula, Scurvy, Skin and Blood Diseases, Eczema, and Sores of all kinds', a local newspaper advertisement encouraged Cotswoldians to part with their cash in exchange for 'Clarke's World-Famed Blood Mixture', 'for cleaning and clearing the blood free of impurities' resulting from 'foul matter of any description'. Talk about a New Year detox (*Evesham Journal & Four Shires Advertiser*).

New Year's Eve December 1961
Woodchester's trusty bell-ringers turned out in 17 degrees of frost to ring in the New Year.

31 December 1782
Time appeared to be finally running out for Thos. Gardiner. The New Year vestry minutes of St Lawrence's record that a warrant was secured against him if he did not 'remove to his own Parish'.

SELECTED SOURCES

Allis's History of Nailsworth, 2nd edn, 1893; Atholl, J., *The Reluctant Hangman: the story of James Berry, executioner, 1884–1892*, 1856; Atkyns, Sir R., *The Ancient and Present State of Glostershire*, 1712; Back, Revd W., *History of Woodchester*, 1972; Baddeley, W. St C., *A Cotteswold Manor: History of Painswick*, 1907; Baker, M.L., *The story of Uley*, 1935; Bartlett, W., *Nineteenth century Stow*, 1911; Bick, D.E., *Old Leckhampton*, 1994; Bigland, R., *1711–1784, Historical, monumental and geneaological collections relative to the County of Gloucester*, facsimile edn, 1990; Blunt, J.H., *Dursley and Its Neighbourhood*, facsimile edn, 1975; Brayne, M., *The Greatest Storm*, 2002; Briggs, K.M., *Folklore of the Cotswolds*, 1974; Bristol and Gloucestershire Archaeological Society, *Transportees from Gloucestershire to Australia 1783–1842*, Irene Wyatt (ed.); Burns, F.D.A., *Heigh for Cotswold! A History of Robert Dover's Olimpick Games*, Robert Dover's Games Society, *c.* 1981; Burrage, H.S., *Baptist Hymn Writers and Their Hymns*, 1888; Buxton, J. (ed.), *Poems of Michael Drayton*, 1953; *Church Bells of Gloucestershire*, Bliss/Sharpe, 1986; Clifford, H., *History of Bourton-on-the-Water*, 1916; Colvin, H.M., *A Biographical Dictionary of English Architects 1660–1840*, 1954; Crawford, O.G.S., *Long Barrows of the Cotswolds*, 1925; Daubeny, U., *Ancient Cotswold Churches*, 1921; Davies, W.H., *The Autobiography of a Super-Tramp*, 1964; Dent, E., *Annals of Winchcombe and Sudeley*, 1877; Derrick, F., *Cotswold Stone*, 1974; Dowler, G., *Gloucestershire Clock and Watch Makers*, 1984; Ellacombe, H.T., *Church Bells of Gloucestershire*, 1881; Fennemore, E.P., *A History of Randwick*, 1893; Fisher, P.H., *1779–1873 Notes and Recollections of Stroud*, facsimile edn, 1975; Fisk, D., *Dr. Jenner of Berkeley*, 1959; *Folk-Lore*, vol. XXIII, 1912; Gloucestershire Archives: various documents; *Gloucestershire Gazette* Centenary Supplement, 'The Progress of Vice exemplified in the life of William Crew of Wotton under Edge'; *Gloucestershire Notes & Queries* – various volumes; Glos. Soc. for Industrial Archaeology Newsletter – July 1965; Hannam-Clark, T., *Drama in Gloucestershire*, 1928; Hodgson, E., *A History of Tetbury*, 1976; Huntley, Revd R.W., *Glossary of Cotswold Dialect*; Hyett, F.A., *Glimpses of the History of Painswick*, 1928; Hyett, Sir F.A., *Supplement Bibliographical Manual of Gloucestershire Literature*, vols 1 & 2, 1915; Hyett, Sir F.A., *The Bibliographer's Manual of Gloucestershire Literature (1895– 97)*; Jeffries J., *Cheese Rolling in Gloucestershire*, 2007; Jewson, N., *By Chance I Did Rove*,

1952; *Kelly's Directory*, 1897; Lee, A.T., *History of the Town and Parish of Tetbury*, 1857; Leland, J., *The Itinerary of John Leland*, L.T. Smith (ed.), 1908; Lewis-Jones, J., *Folklore of the Cotswolds*, 2003; Mace, C.A., *Goode Olde Countree*; Major, N., *Chequers: The Prime Minister's Country House and its History*, 1996; Martell, C., 'Native Apples of Gloucestershire'; Mills, B., *Portrait of Nailsworth*, 2nd edn., 1992; Mills, S., *The Mills of Gloucestershire*, 1989; Moreau, S., *Tour to the Royal Spa at Cheltenham*, 1789; Nutter, C.S., *The Hymns and Hymn Writers of the Church*, 1915; *Oxford Dictionary of National Biography*, various editions, and www.oxforddnb.com; Palmer, R., *Folklore of Gloucestershire*, 2001; Peacock, T.L., *The Genius of the Thames*, 1810; Peerless, J. (ed.), *Tetbury, the place and the people*, 2001; Playne, A.T., *History of the Parishes of Minchinhampton and Avening*, 1915; Reese, P., *The Flying Cowboy: Samuel Cody – Britain's First Airman*, 2006; Richardson, J., *The Local Historian's Encyclopaedia*, 1974; Robinson, T.R. FBHI, 'The Clock Tower at Nailsworth, *The Engineer*, 1953; Roper, I.M., *The Monumental Effigies of Gloucestershire and Bristol*, 1931; Royce, Revd D., *History and Antiquities of Stow*; Rudd, M.A., *Historical Records of Bisley with Lypiatt, Gloucestershire*, 1937; Rudder, S., *A New History of Gloucestershire*, facsimile edn, 1977; Rudkin, M., *The History of Horsley*, 1884; Scott, G.R., *History of Torture Throughout the Ages*; Seddon, Revd W.H., 'Painswick Feast, Its Origin & Meaning', 1921; Sherwood, J., *Oxfordshire by Jennifer Sherwood and Nikolaus Pevsner*, 1974; Sitwell, S., *1897–1988: British Architects and Craftsmen*, 1960; Smythe, F.T., *Chronicles of Shortwood: 1705–1916*, 1916; Stewart, G.O.W., *The Victoria Hall, Bourton-on-the-Water 1897–1976*, 1977; Stoker, B., *1847–1912: Famous Imposters*, 1910; Stratford, J., *Good and Great Men of Gloucestershire*, 1867; *Stroud Chronology & Diary 1360–1869*; Symonds, P.R., *Area Eight In The War Against Hitlerism: being an account of the Civil Defence Services and ARP in Stroud & Nailsworth*, 1945; Taunt, H.W., *The Rollright Stones*; TBGAS – Gloucestershire Barrows, Analysis, Folklore by L.V. Grinsell, 1960; TBGAS – Gloucestershire Barrows, Lists, H. O'Neil and L.V. Grinsell, 1960; TBGAS – 'The Holy Blood of Hayles W St C Baddeley', 1900; 'The Murderers of Gloucestershire: Hangings in Gloucester Prison (and others) 1872–1939', Senior Officer White PRO; *The Register of the Victoria Cross*, compiled & researched for 'This England' by Nora Buzzell, 1981; Tyerman, L., *Life of Rev G. Whitefield*; Verey, D., *Gloucestershire 1: The Cotswolds*, 1999; Warne, Revd W.L., *A Short History of Moreton-in-Marsh*, 1948; Whiting, J.R.S., *Prison Reform in Gloucestershire 1776–1820*, 1975; Willey, R., *The Black Boy School: Stroud, 1844–1914*, 1970.